KB011226

2021 CONSUMER TREND INSIGHTS

First published in the Republic of Korea in November, 2020 by Miraebook Publishing Co.
Second print: Dec. 7, 2020

Copyright © 2020 by Rando Kim
All rights reserved. No part of this book may be reproduced, stored in a retrieval system, or transmitted in any form or by any means, electronic, mechanical, photocopying, recording, scanning or otherwise without permission of the author and publisher.

Inquiries should be addressed to
Miraebook Publishing Co.
5th Fl., Miraeui-chang Bldg., 62-1 Jandari-ro, Mapo-ku, Seoul
Tel : 82-2-325-7556 / email : mbookjoa@naver.com

www.miraebook.co(miraebookjoa.blog.me)
Instagram.com/miraebook
Facebook.com/miraebook

ISBN 978 89 5989 690 5 13320

2021 CONSUMER TREND INSIGHTS

Rando Kim · Miyoung Jeon, Jihye Choi, Hyuang Eun Lee, June Young Lee
Soojin Lee · Youhyun Alex Suh · Jung Yun Kwon · Dahye Han · Hyewon Lee
Translated by Heejin Koo · Proofread by Michel Lamblin

미래의 창

Authors

Rando Kim (김난도)

Rando Kim is a professor in the Dept. of Consumer Science(DCS), Seoul National University(SNU) and the head of Consumer Trend Center(CTC), SNU. As a specialist in consumer behavior and market trend analysis, he has written more than 20 books including *Trend Korea series, Trend China, What Consumers Want*, and *Luxury Korea*. He has also written essay books, *Amor Fati*, *Future and My Job*, and *Youth, It's Painful* which have sold three million copies in 14 countries. He has conducted research projects about consumer needs finding, new product planning, and market trend probing for Korea's major companies like Samsung, LG, SK, CJ, Hyundai Motors, Amore Pacific, Lotte, Fursys, Nongshim, and Coway.

Miyoung Jeon (전미영)

She currently works as a research fellow in the CTC, SNU. She worked as a research analyst at the Samsung Economic Research Institute. She obtained her BA, MA, and PhD degrees in DCS, SNU. She wrote her Ph.D. dissertation and subsequent articles about purchasing behavior and consumer happiness. She received 'The Best Publication Award' from the Korean Society of Consumer Studies in 2008. She is interested in tracking consumer trends in Korea and China as well as big data analysis for new product development and industrial applications.

Jihye Choi (최지혜)

Jihye Choi, Ph.D. in Consumer Science from DCS, SNU, works as a research fellow at CTC. She has participated in many consulting projects with Korea's leading companies such as Samsung and LG, and gives public lectures on consumer trends. She currently teaches consumer behavior and qualitative research methodology at SNU. She contributes many articles and columns to major Korean newspapers and media.

Hyang Eun Lee (이향은)

Hyang Eun Lee is an associate professor in the Dept. of Service Design Engineering, Sungshin Women's University. She has a master's degree in Design Management from Central Saint Martins in London, England and a Ph.D. in Design from the Graduate School of Arts, SNU with a dissertation: "A Study on the Process Model Focused on Experience: Centering on Experience of a Designer Transformed into Intuitive Insight." Her main area of research includes UX trends and user psychology, as well as design and consumption trends. She is working in research and development as regards to innovation in government and corporations.

June Young Lee (이준영)

June Young Lee currently works as an associate professor in Sang-Myung University. He received a doctorate degree in DCS, SNU. He received 'The Best Paper Award' in *The Journal of Consumer Studies.* He worked as a senior researcher in Life Soft Research lab at LG Electronics. He is a laboratory chief of Consumer Research Center in Sang-Myung University.

Soojin Lee (이수진)

Soojin Lee has completed her BA, MA, and Ph.D. course in DCS, SNU. She has been a senior researcher at CTC since 2015. Prior to joining the center, she was a stock market reporter on Maeil Economic TV. As a contributing researcher, she is conducting a number of consulting projects with clients about consumer trends. She won first prize in the Korean Academic Society of Financial Planning symposium. Her studies focus on consumer trends, consumption culture, and family economics.

YouHyun Alex Suh (서유현)

YouHyun Alex Suh graduated from Central Saint Martins College of Art & Design Textile BA (Hons) in London, UK. She received an MS degree from the Graduate School of Culture Technology, Korea Advanced Institute of Science (KAIST), specializing in design management and consumer behavior. She currently is senior researcher at CTC, and a Ph.D. candidate at SNU, specializing in data-driven trend analysis.

Jung Yoon Kwon (권정윤)

Jeong Yun Kwon is a PhD candidate in DCS, SNU and is currently a senior researcher at CTC. She academically explored the changes in consumers' lives caused by technological change through her master thesis, "Consumer Happiness and Social Comparisons on SNS in Experiential and Material Purchases." Her interests include rapidly changing modern society, its impact on consumer cultures, and various research methodologies to capture them.

Dahye Han (한다혜)

Dahye Han received a BA in the Department of Psychology, SNU and an M.A. degree in DCS, SNU. Currently, she is doing her Ph.D. at SNU and works as a researcher in CTC. With her masters thesis, "A Study on Consumer Emotion Changes in Online Clothing Purchasing Process," her research interests focus on consumer behavior, trend analysis, and consumption psychology.

Hyewon Lee (이혜원)

Hyewon Lee has worked at Dasan Books, and Kakao Page Corp. for over 15 years. She has an MA degree with her thesis: "Comparative Analysis of Age Effect, Period Effect and Cohort Effect - Focusing on Consumer Perception Toward CSR." She is currently interested in quantifying consumer behavior, especially generational theory or cohort analysis in the digital media environment.

Consumer Trend Center, Seoul National University

Consumer Trend Center (CTC) was established in 2004 for the analysis of rapidly changing consumer trends and has announced "ten trend keywords" every year since 2007. CTC has done collaborative research with many companies, and provided education programs about consumer needs analysis. CTC plans to be incorporated with the consulting firm, "The Trend Korea Company," which specializes in trend forecasting, generation studies, marketing planning, and new product/service development.

Preface

We have published a new book on *Consumer Trend Insights* each year since 2008, summarizing Korea's annual consumer trends with keywords. And for each of those 13 years, the books have grabbed the No. 1 spot on the domestic bestseller list without fail, a measure of the support shown by our avid readers. We have come to realize that the keywords highlighted in our *Consumer Trend Insights* series are not only an analysis of the Korean market, but also universal trends that reflect the global market. We deemed it was high time to provide our global readers with our keen perception of social changes and publish an English version in 2019 for the 2020 edition of the book. This is our second English translation in the series.

The outbreak of COVID-19 at the outset of 2020 threw the whole world into chaos. Mandatory masks were just the first step in adapting to the new normal. Protracted social distancing obviously led to a global recession and impacted all aspects of our daily lives, such as working, studying, eating, drinking and traveling. Our lives changed dramatically. These trends, which have undergone secondary and tertiary transitions, are massively transforming the world's culture, politics, economy, and society.

As a trend analyst, the question I received most often was: "How will COVID-19 change trends?" And our analysis of changes in 2020's global consumer trends, based on our 12 years of research, has led us to the following conclusion:

"Coronavirus will not change the direction of trends, but it will impact their speed."

In other words, the pandemic has quickened the pace of polarization, intensifying trends that were on the rise, and diminishing keywords that were waning. Just take a look at online and mobile purchases, teleworking, and homeschooling, which are now mainstream—a drastic change from pre-COVID days when they were being introduced. What would have previously taken three to four years to implement has taken less than six months. The moral of this crisis is that we need to swiftly respond to changing trends. Once we move forward, we can't go back. Our best and only option is to closely examine today's trends and to make meticulous adjustments in response.

In the past twelve years, our *Consumer Trend Insights* books outlined keywords to represent the following year's trends, with the first letters of the keyword phrases forming an acronym that represented the animal of that year in the Chinese zodiac. For example, 2020 was the year of the rat, hence our acronym "MIGHTY MICE." The acronym for 2021 is "COWBOY HERO," in the hopes that we will be able to put the coronavirus under control, just as cowboys tame the bucking bull. We expect our healthcare workers, with their sacrifices and dedication, as well as our civic-minded public, will all emerge as the true heroes in our struggle against the outbreak.

It gives me great pleasure to acknowledge those who have helped us with this book. First of all, I am grateful to the voluntary trend hunters, "Trenders Nal"' for their collection of useful trend artifacts which helped define our ten keywords. I particularly want to thank Heejin Koo for her translation and Professor Michel Lamblin, Professor Na Yuri, and YouHyun Alex Suh for their proofreading. The translation process was a tough challenge because the original Korean text used many newly-coined terms in the Korean language and from a particular cultural context. Despite many issues, they made succinct translations and interpretations within a time constraint. I would like to express a special thanks to CEO Euihyun Sung and the staff of Miraebook Publishing Co., who encouraged me to publish an English version of the book. Lastly, I have to thank my co-authors who generated great ideas and first drafts of trend keywords. This book would not have been possible without their hard work and dedication.

COVID-19 and its uncertainties may have shaken the global market to its core, but in truth such changes were in the offing for the past decade. In other words, if we had anticipated such trends ahead of time, we could have turned this crisis into an opportunity. We hope that our ten keywords listed in this book will serve as a compass for global organizers, developers, promoters and managers to better identify constant changes in the market and among their consumers, not just in Korea but also for the world at large.

Rando Kim
Professor, Department of Consumer Science
Seoul National University
Seoul, November, 2020

CONTENTS

COWBOY HERO

COMING OF "V-NOMICS"

The global spread of COVID-19 has forced us to confront a brave new world. What are the economic and consumer changes triggered by the outbreak and their implications going forward? The 'V' in our first keyword is for "virus," and "V-nomics" signifies "an economy transformed by the virus." We pose the following four questions: (1) Is a V-shaped recovery possible? (2) What kind of changes can we expect within the "untact" trend, accelerated by the coronavirus? (3) How will consumer values fluctuate amid the crisis? (4) What vision do we need to tackle this era of V-nomics? Predicting the future always involves walking a fine line between the possible and the impossible. Still, we would like to answer the above questions as follows: (1) We will likely see a generally polarized K-shaped recovery, but different economic sectors may exhibit V, U, W and S-type recoveries as well. (2) The "untact" trend will settle on a golden ratio between "face-to-face" and "remote" contact, and we will likely see organizational structuring focus more on performance-driven KPI (key performance index), education gravitating toward "blended or flipped learning," and retail aimed at maximizing "customer experience." (3) Customer values will shift toward dependable brands and companies that strive toward coexistence, and will show a qualitative change based on increased interest in environmental protection and "substance." And finally, in order to cope with the severe polarization triggered by the pandemic, societies will rely more on a sense of community spirit, bringing to the fore the importance of the role of government and the versatility of an organization's capacity to adapt to change.

Everyone is required to wear masks in public; we cannot go to school or the office; overseas travel has become a memory only found in photo albums; internet cafés, karaoke rooms and clubs have closed down; and crowded shopping malls are a thing of the past.

How would the world have reacted to such a sci-fi movie released back in 2019? The common response would have likely been, "Unrealistic, even for a work of fiction," or "Would that even be possible in an age of cutting-edge science and technology?" And yet, these unbelievable events have become our reality. COVID-19 is a black hole that has entirely absorbed all areas of the world, including politics, the economy, society and culture. The virus, which began spreading in January 2020, quickly reached all corners of the world, resulting in countless infections and deaths. The number of confirmed patients exceeded 20 million as of August 12, three times the total 6.7 million cases of the highly pathogenic flu that gripped the world in 2007. Its mortality rate of 3.6 percent is 12 times that of the 2007 flu of 0.3

percent.[1]

People in general are trying to put on a brave face and adapt to the new normal, but they find it difficult to shake off their anxiety and fear. What lies ahead? We have no timeframe for a viable coronavirus vaccine to reach the market. British medical scientist Sir Mark Walport grimly said in an interview with BBC that coronavirus "is going to be with us forever in some form or another." Currently there are no certain predictions for an end to the virus's spread, but nevertheless we need to determine the course of consumer and economic trends shaken by the outbreak. The silver lining is that humanity has always found a way, even in crises worse than the one we face today. Humans adapt quickly to change. Its impact will likely allow mankind to approach the problem from new perspectives and provide a springboard into the future.

How will COVID-19 change the consumer market in 2021? At the time of writing this book, trends remain in drastic flux, and yet we still need to assess a course for the future by analyzing all angles of changes seen so far. In that respect, we propose "V-nomics" as the first trending keyword. The 'V' is for "virus," with "V-nomics" signifying "an economy transformed by the virus." More importantly, it is the basis for answers to the questions we are most anxious about. The questions are as follows:

(1) Can we see an economic rebound, such as a V-shaped

recovery? (2) What kind of variations can we expect within the "untact" (a term coined and popularized by the Trend Korea Company, meaning "non-contact") trend, accelerated by the coronavirus? (3) How will consumer values change? (4) What vision do we need to persevere in this era of V-nomics?

It so happens that each of these questions contains a word starting with 'V.' Let us suggest some answers to the "4V" questions posed above.

Q1. Is a V-shaped Recovery Possible?

— Wide variation is likely amid K-shaped polarization

The economy is gravely and rapidly shrinking. MERS, SARS and the avian flu have all come and gone, but none were as brutal as the current crisis. As mankind's survival hangs on the balance, the impact on the world's economy is just as detrimental. In fact, economic indicators around the world have posted their worst ever records. Indices for consumer confidence, consumer prices and economic growth have dipped into the red. Economies around the world, including South Korea's, are shaken by the catastrophe. Many have predicted a "90 percent economy," even with a post-COVID recovery. The "90 percent economy" was coined by British weekly The Economist, meaning that economic activity worldwide, including consumption, employment and production, will operate at only 90 percent of normal levels. Even a 1 percent decline in growth is detrimental to the street economy, let alone a shocking 10 percent contraction. Many analysts have predicted that Korea will see its first negative growth since it shrank by 5.1 percent during the financial crisis of 1998.

So, the biggest question is: will we see a rebound in 2021? Yes, in terms of numbers. The OECD's outlook for Korea's economic growth stood at 3.1 percent for 2021. At first glance, a V-shaped recovery seems possible, but not everything is coming up roses. Since the year-on-year growth depends on the previous year, the 2020 economy will greatly affect the so-called base effect. The more detrimental the performance for 2020, the greater the rebound will seem in 2021, causing an illusory effect. Central and regional governments have injected funds to boost the economy, but deposits in the first half of 2020 surged by a whopping 109 trillion won ($94 billion).[2] This implies that "revenge saving" increased more than "revenge spending." Companies and households inevitably chose to save up for a rainy day, rather than spending or investing.

As consumers and businesses closely watch their spending and investments, we should carefully examine patterns of recovery by each sector and industry, rather than focus on an overall V-shaped recovery. Opinions vary on the shape of the future rally. A V-shape implies a steep rebound; a

<K-shape recovery>

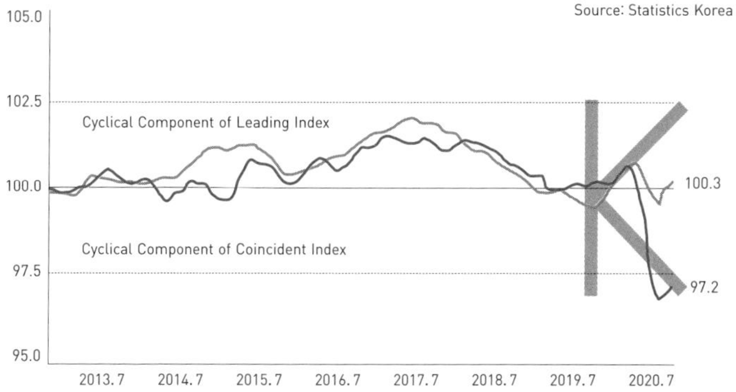

U-shape suggests that the economy will remain depressed for a longer period; an L-shape indicates a long-term recession; a W-shape means a fluctuation between growth and contraction; and a "swoosh-shape", as in the Nike logo, signifies a gradual recovery following a sharp decline. However, the most recent and plausible explanation is a "K-shape,"[3] which would be a polarized phenomenon with an upward recovery and a downward recession occurring at the same time. Take for example the figures for industrial output released in July 2020 by Statistics Korea통계청, which show monthly gains in the manufacturing index of 21.5 percent and 14.4 percent in June and July that year, as well as steady increases in other sectors. On the other hand, the index for the service sector slipped gradually, posting year-on-year contractions of 5 percent, 6.1 percent, 0.1 percent and 1.3 percent in March through July in 2020, showing a typical K-shape.[4]

Expectations for an economic rebound remain high, but a "real recovery" will likely be slow and form a K-shape. The Cyclical Component of Leading Index has bounced back to 100.3 to pre-pandemic levels of above 100, whereas the Cyclical Component of Coincident Index still hovers below 100 at 97.2. The Cyclical Component of Leading Index provides a short-term economic outlook and recovery, whereas the Cyclical Component of Coincident Index offers a snapshot of the current economic cycle. These two indices, which used to similarly track one another, started to diverge in March 2020 at the height of the pandemic. This implies that the expectation for a recovery is high, but the actual rebound fails to meet such hopes. In fact, the hardest hit by the outbreak are small business owners who are the backbone of the street economy. According to a Federation of Korean Industries report that surveyed 22 of the nation's associations and unions for small businesses, the performance outlook for the second half of 2020 saw a 42 percent decline and a steeper 52.6 percent slump should the pandemic worsen, yet another illustration of a K-shape.[5]

The U.S. economy, during three economic recessions, saw stocks for the top 25 percent businesses gain 6 percent, whereas those of the bottom 25 percent fell 44 percent. Frankly speaking, a K-shaped polarized recovery may well be an inevitable feature of capitalism.[6] However, a drastic effect on the economy, including disasters such as a viral outbreak, tends to escalate the process. While the "K" represents the overall shape, when seen through a magnifying glass its trajectory can rise, dip and fluctuate. Let's take a closer look at the five variations that we may see exhibited in numerous sectors.

(1) A V-shape represents a steep rebound; (2) a U-shape suggests a longer recession; (3) a W-shape indicates a fluctuation, as seen in correlation with social distancing measures; (4) an S-shape shows an acceleration of an already existing rally; and (5) an upside-down V-shape signifies flash gains that capitalize on the pandemic.

These five types vary depending on, firstly, the level of face-to-face contact. A higher level of direct contact increases risk during a pandemic. The second criterion is about what kind of substitutes exist. For example, one can substitute buying bottled water at a nearby supermarket with ordering it online. When your favorite bar shuts down, you can always buy wine from a nearby convenience store. Still, drinking alone can never replace the ambience created by being with friends and loved ones. When establishments are allowed to open once again, people will head to them to enjoy their nightlife. This indicates that a complete substitute is not possible, which can lead to a faster recovery. And the third factor relates to how the recovery coincides with existing trends. "Untact" or at-home purchases were already

<Types of economic recovery according to the characteristics of each industry hit>

Types		characteristics	industry
V-shape	Steep recovery	High level of face-to-face contact; Low level of substitutes	Theme parks, hair salons, musicals, local hospitals (internal medicine, pediatrics, dentists, etc.) convenience stores in business districts, at-home services (home-study materials, housekeeping, etc.)
U-shape	Gradual recovery	High level of face-to-face contact; High level of substitutes	Overseas travel, duty-free shopping, plastic surgery (for international patients), karaoke rooms, gyms, major supermarket chains, hotels catering to businesspeople and tourists, formal attire
W-shape	Fluctuation	High level of face-to-face contact; Sensitive to social distancing measures	Public transportation, restaurants, cafés, bars, theaters, malls and arcades, department stores, specially located convenience stores
S-shape	Acceleration	Coincides with "untact" trends	Online shopping, delivery services, camping-related industries, hotels and resorts catering to domestic clientele, golf-related industries, at-home workouts, home meal replacements (HMR), over-the-top (OTT) media services, convenience stores in residential areas, home improvement and DIY, athleisure wear, health supplements

rising trends that further accelerated due to the spread of the virus. Such sectors will likely continue to grow even after the end of the pandemic. However, if the sector saw a brief jump in sales on the back of the outbreak with no correlation to existing trends, then it will see a sharp decline. We can draw up the following chart for the five recovery shapes, applying the above conditions and sales of the first three quarters of 2020.

1. V-shape: Steep recovery

These sectors will likely suffer from initial losses due to their high level of face-to-face contact. However, due to their lack of substitutes, they are expected to recover quickly once the infection dies down. For example, patients are refraining from visiting dentists, internal medicine and pediatric clinics, but once the situation improves, they will return. At-home services, such as tutoring, home-study materials, and housekeeping, declined over concerns about letting in outside guests but will likely see a V-shaped recovery. Color cosmetics will also see a similar rebound once the pandemic ebbs and people stop wearing masks. Theme parks and hair salons will likely see their customers return quickly, and audiences will return to theaters to watch

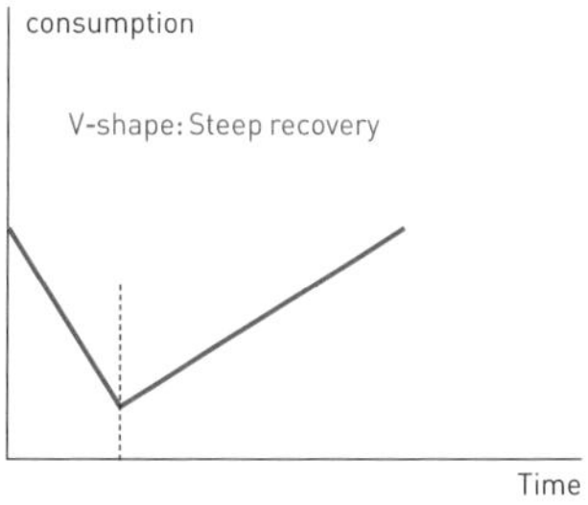

musicals as they cannot be enjoyed in nearly the same way on TV at home.

2. U-shape: Gradual recovery

These businesses were hit hard by the pandemic because of their high level of face-to-face contact, as well as the various substitutes available. Recovery will likely be more gradual even when the crisis is reined in, if the need for services or purchases is not urgent, or if effects from the pandemic continue to persist. Overseas tours, duty-free shops, hotels catering to businesspeople and international tourists, and plastic surgery clinics focusing on overseas patients, all belong to this category. Major supermarket chains yielded to online shopping malls, while karaoke rooms and fitness centers were profoundly affected by mandates restricting their operations. Convenience stores at specialized locations and formalwear makers will also take longer to recover as more people work from home.

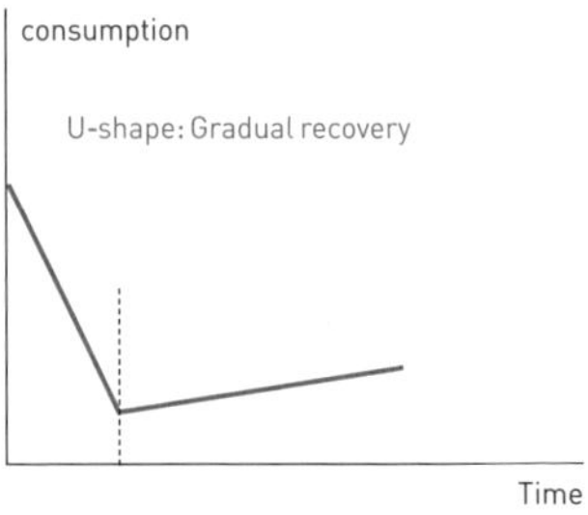

3. W-shape: Fluctuation

This category includes businesses with high levels of face-to-face contact and that are particularly sensitive to social

Malls and arcades that spread over massive areas show a quintessential W-shaped recovery. They will most likely bounce back faster than any other sectors once the pandemic reaches its end.

distancing measures. It differs from the U-shaped recovery, in that these businesses have become a part of our everyday lives and therefore will likely see a faster rebound once governments ease preventative measures. Public transportation, restaurants, cafés, bars and theaters belong in this category. Over-the-top (OTT) services can replace theaters but many still want to go on dates to feel the sensory impact of surround sound and the big screen at the cinema. Malls and arcades differ from major supermarket

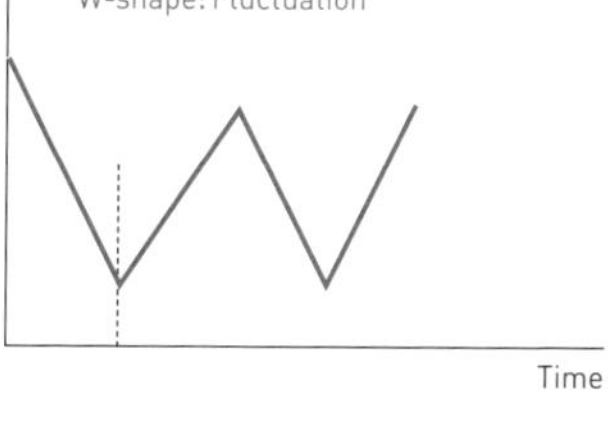

chains in that they have a built-in element of entertainment, rather than just functioning as selling points for daily necessities. Convenience stores located in specialized areas also belong to this category. These sectors will likely see an immediate recovery once the preventative and social distancing measures are normalized.

4. S-shape: Acceleration

This category coincides with "untact" trends. Its growth, already on an upward trajectory before the outbreak, catapulted with the spread of the virus. Untact retailers such as online shopping malls and delivery services, camping and golf-related goods and services, as well as hotels and resorts catering to domestic clientele (which had seen a steady rise in customers) took advantage of the outbreak. The increase in those staying and working from home prompted gains in sectors related to at-home workouts, home meal replacements (HMR), OTT media service, and convenience stores located in residential areas. The reason why they are not included in the upside-down V-shaped recovery is because they will likely continue to see growth even after the end of the pandemic.

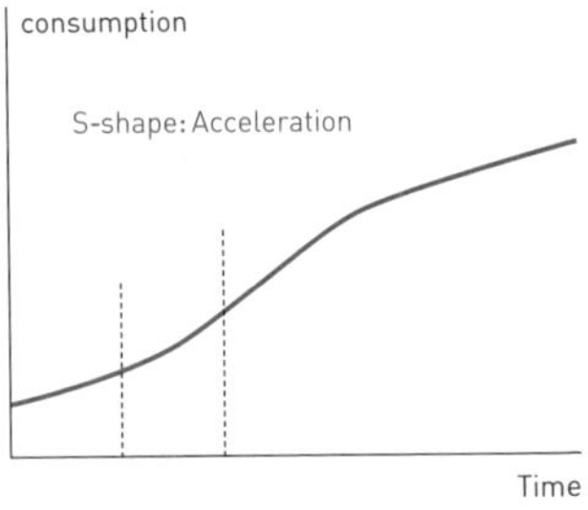

5. Upside-down V: Flash gains that capitalize on COVID-19

This kind of recovery capitalizes on the outbreak through "reflective demand" and "retaliation purchases." Video communications surged as more people worked and attended school from home, prompting similar gains in personal computer and tablet PC sales. Also included in this section: domestic tours and luxury goods purchases, which serve as alternatives to overseas travel; home furniture, large-screen TVs and projectors, which jumped in demand as more people stayed indoors; esthetics and skincare products used to treat skin abrasions from masks; plastic surgery (for domestic patients) on the back of the increase in remote WFH (work from home) video conferencing; and even psychiatric therapy for the increase in people suffering the "Corona blues." In fashion, home wear, lounge wear, and "one-mile wear" (the comfortable clothing worn within a mile radius of one's home) were all the rage as people spent more time at home. These products and services will not likely slump immediately after the pandemic comes to an end, but their growth won't be as stellar as during the pandemic, a clear difference from sectors in the S-shaped upturn.

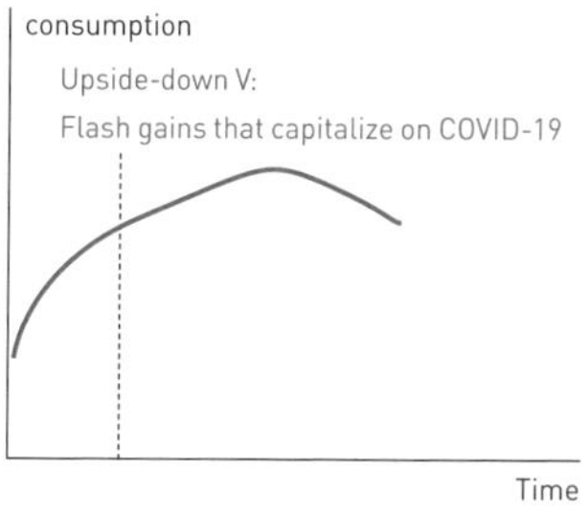

Q2. What Kind of Variations Can We Expect in the "Untact" Trend?

— Finding the most efficient golden ratio of face-to-face

"Untact" became a pandemic catchword in Korea, indicating the elimination of contact between people. When we used the term in our 2018 edition of Consumer Trend Insights, in reference to kiosks and smartphone app economic trends, we did not have "social distancing" in mind. However, regardless of the intent, the untact lifestyle is becoming an essential part of our daily routine. When Amazon, the leader among U.S. online retailers, announced that it may take over closed spaces left by failing department stores such as Sears and J.C. Penny and use them as distribution warehouses, it had huge implications. It demonstrated how the pandemic entrenched the idea of "untact" in our lives. So, the question is, how will this untact trend change in the future? Let's take a closer look at teleworking, homeschooling, and untact retail, the three areas most related to this trend.

Outlook for teleworking

The pandemic has forced companies to introduce more flexible working policies, including teleworking, staggered hours, as well as selective and flexible work schedules. Teleworking in particular was a new system that many companies were forced to adopt. Zoom Video Communications emerged as the Cinderella in this coronavirus tale. Even before the outbreak, the medium-sized company posted solid growth with daily users of 10 million. Its shares were listed on NASDAQ in 2019 but remained a relatively unfamiliar name. However, the pandemic thrust the company into the limelight, with daily users exploding 20-fold to 200 million. Such new services, incorporating the latest in technology, have even changed corporate hiring practices. The Samsung Group, South Korea's top conglomerate, held online recruitment exams for the first time in its 63-year history. Major banks have modified their hiring processes to include both regular and rolling recruitment. Though the desperate measures may have been born out of negative factors, they have some positive aspects such as providing an opportunity to eliminate existing inefficiencies related to the recruitment process. An SK Telecom survey found that 63.7 percent of its employees considered the policy "helpful in increasing or maintaining work efficiency," while 34 percent found it "rather uncomfortable, but manageable," resulting in overall positive feedback of 97 percent.[7]

But this does not mean that all aspects of teleworking are positive. It is inefficient for teams that require collaboration, and accuracy is lost when members fail to "read between the lines." The separation of work and personal lives is no longer possible, giving rise to issues therein. So how would teleworking change after the outbreak becomes more manageable? The system will likely evolve into an organized combination of face-to-face and remote arrangements, depending on the tasks involved. The job's key performance index (KPI) will likely determine where and how they work. KPI measures how effectively a company is achieving its key business objectives. Teleworking and flexible work schedules are possible when the tasks can be measured in terms of performance. However, jobs that require collective decisions and creativity through collaboration, or a more comprehensive KPI, may initially find multiple work shifts and working off-site more suitable, but may ultimately find it more productive to come to the office.

SmartStudy스마트스터디, creator of Baby Shark and Pinkfong animations, is a great example. Ever since the outbreak, it recommended all of its employees to telecommute. Currently 60 percent of its employees choose to telework, while 40 percent come to the office, leaving the decision up to the staff on where they feel they can work most productively. Its policies, such as teleworking, unlimited paid leaves, flexible working schedules and funding for working dinners and office supplies, may seem lax, but there is one rule that trumps all: everyone should achieve results.[8] Such policies boosted company sales 11-fold, and its operating profits 23-fold, in the past five years. SmartStudy's model shows us that blindly introducing a teleworking environment may be counter-productive without the support of the relevant corporate culture or the application of performance-oriented tasks.

Outlook for online education

Korea's education system was forced to start the school year online for the first time in its history. Parents, students and teachers went through growing pains as they were thrown into a new paradigm of online education. However, friendships cannot develop through WiFi. Kids should play on school grounds, and university students should learn as much as they can through extracurricular activities and in lecture halls. Schools will likely return to normal faster than the workplace once we see an end to the pandemic. Still, learning methods will not likely revert completely to a pre-COVID-19 system. "Blended learning," based on classroom lectures and supplemented by online lessons, will likely become standard. A survey of 2,000 elementary, middle and high school teachers in July 2000 showed that 56.9 percent agreed that blended learning will eventually become the accepted method.[9] This approach effectively combines the strengths of two different systems through relevant application. A mixture of online and offline activities such as face-to-face classes and online studies are typical of this method.

Seoul National University, Korea University and KAIST (Korea Advanced Institute of Science and Technology) had already introduced the "flipped learning" method before the pandemic, applying a "reverse learning" system in lectures.

Schools may not revert completely back to offline classrooms from online lectures once COVID-19 recedes. A "blended learning" that incorporates both will likely become standard.

Students prep for their courses with video and reading materials provided by professors, then hold discussions or solve tasks during their lectures. Such a method was already introduced in some of their courses, allowing professors and students to ease into an online format. Educational efficiency will likely be maximized by combining offline, online, and flipped learning. Elementary, middle and high schools are focusing more on blended learning because supplementing courses with online lectures compensates for face-to-face classes that are sometimes limited by time and space. On the other hand, lessons within the classroom make up for online classes' drawbacks, such as the loss of human contact, fears about learning by oneself, and the resulting loss of motivation.

Outlook for untact retail

2020 was a banner year for online retailers. As outlined in S-shaped recovery, an already growing sector could spread its wings in the turbulent winds of COVID-19. Online untact (or "ontact") trade is expected to expand its market share beyond the pandemic. Still, as we saw in the case of teleworking and education, online retail will likely combine several formats to try and reach an optimal structure.

The first is "strengthening the untact factor." Lotte Mart increased the number of its unattended cash registers at its Seocho branch in Seoul from 10 to 22 following the outbreak. Drive-throughs have become a staple, not just for COVID testing, but also in all sectors ranging from fast food and coffee shops, to hotels, libraries, convenience stores, department stores, and even fisheries markets. The service will likely expand even after the outbreak subsides as vendors seek to cut down on serving time, improve convenience, save labor costs and minimize the burden of human contact.

The second format will likely supplement its untact operations with a dash of a human element. Customers can sample products on their own at Amorepacific's "Untact Zone" at Lotte Department Store's branch in Cheongnyang-ni, eastern Seoul, as well as receive beauty and make-up tips from helpful staff at its next-door "Counseling Zone." The company divided their space to cater to their younger clientele who do not wish to be bothered while shopping, and to their older customers who want a more personal service and guidance before making their purchase.

A service model that combines untact and human elements has also appeared in the market. Wonders원더스, a delivery startup, introduced its "same-day arrival service" for smartphones. When a customer orders a smartphone online, the delivery staff not only deliver the device but also take care of the registration and other documentation necessary to open an account – the same service you would receive at a mobile phone dealership. What is crucial is that the deliverer completes the task within 20 minutes of arrival. Even if face-to-face meetings are unavoidable, the system minimizes contact while maintaining the advantages of an online purchase. The company dubs the service "the experiential delivery" and Kim Chang-soo, CEO of Wonders defines it as a "middle-contact," or "middletact" service.[10] "Middletact" tries to find a comfortable balance between "untact" and "human" services and is expected to maximize experiential value in face-to-face deliveries.

So, how can an offline retailer survive amid an evolution of untact sales channels? The answer lies in how to provide customers with a unique experience that differs from online shopping. This includes an overwhelming sense of space, the physical product itself, and the element of experience. Starfield Library별마당 도서관, within the COEX Mall, has been cited on numerous occasions as an example for its overwhelming dimensions, which drew visitors back to its space. Samsung Electronics' offline Digital Plaza merged smaller branches to provide bigger showrooms for customers to use and experience their devices, maximizing the physical element for the buyers' experience, managing to lure them back to its stores.

Q3. How Will Consumer Values Change?

— Preference for dependable brands, focus on coexistence, the environment and "substance"

COVID-19 has transformed consumer trends not just in quantity but also in quality, shifting preferences and values in purchases. When faced with a crisis, customers instinctively seek out dependable and trustworthy goods. The pandemic is swaying consumer standards for choosing products, thus resulting in a rush for No.1 brands. For example, choices for staples such as instant noodles (ramyeon), microwave rice and tuna, were heavily tilted toward leading brands rather than newer up-and-coming ones. Consumers tend to minimize risk by choosing dependable popular brands amid the current disaster and economic downturn.

It's not just because these products are market favorites: undoubtedly, consumers expect these established brands and companies to better cope with a crisis than their competition. According to consulting firm McKinsey's survey of 2,500 consumers in the U.S., U.K., France and Germany, more than 40 percent changed their brand preferences according to the company's pricing, available inventory, online purchasing ability, and strategies dealing with the outbreak.[11]

Brands and companies that share the pain

Consumers are more favorable toward and feel secure about companies that actively take steps to deal with a crisis. They prefer companies and brands that maintain or even raise salaries of their employees and try to support their welfare, despite having to halt operations as part of the government's shutdown mandate. McKinsey cited the example of Lululemon, a maker of athleisure specializing in yoga and other sports apparel. When the company had to temporarily shut down stores in Europe and North America in March 2020, it set aside $2 million to help out employees and managers who were hit by the crisis. Their staff, a.k.a. "ambassadors," were able to weather these difficulties with the support and security provided by the company.

A CEO's capability shines through when dealing with apprehension caused by the pandemic. Facebook's Mark Zuckerberg handed out a $1,000 bonus to each one of his 45,000 employees in March 2020 to help them weather the storm during troubling times. The bonus was deemed as "compensation" for employees who missed out on benefits such as using the company cafeteria and other amenities because they were working from home. Each employee also received an "exceeds expectations" rating for the first six-month review of 2020, quickly reassuring its workers who were anxious about how teleworking would affect their performance assessments. The company's stock price and corporate image had suffered due to a string of privacy breaches and fake news scandals, but its CEO's swift response to the outbreak was hailed as a positive corporate example in times of crisis. In Korea, Hyundai Department Store set a similar example. The retailer handed out bonuses of 1 million won ($820) to each of the 3,000 store managers of small and medium-sized brands, a total of 3 billion won ($2.5 million), and also slashed commission rates and maintenance fees for small and medium food and beverage sellers in their department stores. It also handed out payments five months in advance for small and medium-sized vendors and suppliers. Such efforts illustrate how a company tries to share the burden with its suppliers, stakeholders and its employees in times of crisis. As illustrated, consumers will likely keep track of a company's social responsibility even after the pandemic.

Consumer interest in sustainability

Businesses need to transform to achieve consumer recognition in terms of their environmental, social, and corporate governance practices. These three, dubbed "ESG," are central factors that sway investment and purchases, and include not just the company's sales and operating profits, but also its sensitivities toward the environment, staff treatment, as well as transparency in business and corporate governance. Investment figures attest to this trend. Morningstar, which evaluates global funds, reported that investments in equity funds declined since the start of the pandemic, and yet ESG funds saw $71 billion in new investments. The number of new ESG funds surged from 60 in 2015 to the current 400. Consumers and society as a whole are constantly monitoring companies that wreak havoc on the environment. ExxonMobil, the U.S. energy giant which once had the world's largest market cap, was shunned by investors after its intentional plans not to take part in global efforts to cut down on greenhouse gas emissions were revealed. Its stock price plunged from $80 to around $30 and ExxonMobil suffered the indignity of being kicked out from the Dow Jones Industrial Average for the first time in 92 years. In contrast, Denmark's state-run DONG Energy sold off its fossil fuel operations altogether, changed its name to Ørsted and reinvented itself as a leading developer of offshore wind energy. Its stock, which stood at around 270 krone ($31) in 2016, recently more than tripled to 850 krone ($134).[12] Such is the virtuous cycle in which ethical companies show performance gains.

Focus on the fundamentals

Instability induced by the pandemic has also triggered a rise in eco-friendly purchases and interest in "substance." When time stands still due to a viral outbreak, humanity takes a long hard look at the severity of environmental pollution caused by human excess. Changes in people's perception are evident following the outbreak. An April 2020 survey of 1,000 people above the age of 20 showed that 53 percent had shifted their life values to focus more on "examining a future for me and my family" following the pandemic, while 41 percent said the outbreak "provided an opportunity to look back on their view of life."[13] COVID-19 has prompted us to focus more on the fundamentals.

"I like baseball and thought it wouldn't be much fun to watch a game without spectators. But I found that I liked it better because once you remove distractions such as cheering and the spectators' expressions, you get to concentrate more on the game itself."

— A 30-year-old female graduate student speaking at a consumer interview at the SNU Consumer Trend Center.

As this baseball fan points out, she was able to focus more on the game itself after the outbreak. Likewise, the attack of the virus in 2020 allowed consumers to focus more on "substance." That is, they have an increased need for a "core" which remains true and faithful to life's fundamentals. A survey by Korea Research한국리서치 showed that since the epidemic, consumer sensitivity to a brand's safety and quality and other fundamental aspects has increased, as opposed to any concern for peripheral events, discounts or promotions.[14] For example, according to an analysis of health and beauty chain CJ Olive Young's sales in the midst of the pandemic from May 29 to June 2 of 2020, the biggest selling product was toner, the first step in skincare, which was up 60 percent from a year earlier. Toners are essential to rebalance the skin, provide moisture and are the basis of a skincare routine after washing away dirt and makeup. The need for color cosmetics slumped because consumers have either refrained from going outdoors or started wearing masks, in contrast to the rising demand for basic skincare products. Consumer day-to-day trends are also focusing on the basics such as health and hygiene, rather than a colorful outward appearance.

Q4. What Vision Do We Need?

— Outlook and Implications

Infectious disease pandemics are unique in many ways. The virus may not play favorites, but the probability of exposure is not always equal. Social conditions are closely related to the virus's cause, process and end result. All of these shapes are one aspect of the "corona divide." The K-shape is not limited to a subset of an economic recovery but is also evident in our individual daily lives.

Data for Korea shows that the valley of polarization is widening. Statistics Korea's survey of household trends in the first quarter showed that household incomes slightly increased year-on-year, with the figure for households in the bottom 10 percent of the earning bracket slipping 3.6 percent year-on-year to 959,019 won ($829). The P90/P10 ratio, which illustrates the income disparity between the top 10 percent and bottom 10 percent of earners, has grown even wider from pre-coronavirus figures. The pandemic slashed jobs held by low-income households, including gig and temporary workers, while assets held by higher-income households increased in value in a market with excess liquidity.

Be wary of a "winner-takes-all" world

As pointed out by political philosopher and Harvard University professor Michael Sandel, the crisis has magnified problems that existed even before the outbreak. Social and structural issues inherent in our society have resurfaced in the midst of COVID-19. The ability to respond to the acceleration of digital transformation varies widely between those who are prepared and those who aren't. Homeschooling and teleworking have expanded the digital scope in our lives, reinforcing a winner-takes-all structure. Learning from home is not feasible for households without a personal computer or parental support. According to a report by the Korea Education and Research Information Service, an arm of the Education Ministry, 79 percent of teachers noted that the learning gap widened after introducing the homeschooling format.[15]

Polarization among suppliers has also worsened. As online classes are becoming available to all, students and viewers are more likely to flock to content that is superior in quality. MasterClass, known as the Netflix of online classes, is rising in popularity, showcasing premium lectures by renowned celebrities such as Natalie Portman on acting, Martin Scorsese on directing, and Stephen Curry on basketball.

A Korean film school professor at a private university confessed that "in an era where we can attend lectures on films by Martin Scorsese and Park Chan-wook, I have to wonder about my competitive edge."[16] Such trends will likely expand in the future. The "Rule of Three" may have been the rule of thumb in an offline market, where the top three competitors take the lion's share. In an online-centric world of V-nomics, a "Rule of One," in which the winner takes all, will likely prevail.

So, what can we do in an era of COVID-19 that exacerbates social sacrifices? The immediate task is to survive while adhering to preventative measures against the virus's spread.

However, it should be based on a virtue of generosity. According to a National Human Rights Commission of Korea survey in April 2020, 91 percent of respondents said that ever since the outbreak, they empathized with the view that "I could be the subject of discrimination" if they caught the virus, which even outweighed their worry of actually catching the virus. And 69 percent recognized that some people had been targets of hatred and discrimination at the peak of the pandemic.[17]

Such instances of social injustice and discrimination become major hurdles in resolving issues amid instability. According to a study by Paul van Lange, a professor of psychology at Vrije Universiteit Amsterdam, we obtain the emotional energy necessary to maintain social cooperation through the generosity of others, or in other words, through selfless acts of kindness. We are able to practice self-restraint and refrain from deviant and antisocial behavior by observing such altruistic actions for others.

"Adapt or Die"

The role of government is crucial in V-nomics. A government's function grows ever enormous as disinfection and preventative measures have become top priorities. Drones whizz overhead in the U.S. issuing warnings, China enforces the wearing of masks through facial recognition technology, while Hong Kong requires anyone arriving from overseas to wear a wristband that tracks the wearer's location. There are privacy and human rights concerns regarding the overwhelming power wielded by government with the abuse of surveillance technology, reminiscent of "Big Brother." The government's efforts to encourage spending and to boost the economy by injecting funds are absolutely necessary. Still, there is rising doubt about national debt levels and efficacy in the distribution of relief funds. The crux of the matter lies in avoiding the temptation to exert excessive authority and finding the right balance during the recovery process. Government needs to reflect on how best to share the responsibility along with consumers and businesses to resolve issues together rather than believing that it must solve everything.

The responsibility of businesses and organizations in an era of V-nomics lies in fostering the ability to swiftly respond to changing trends based on a vision for the future. As outlined in Chapter Four entitled "Best We Pivot," survival depends on adaptability. This is not just applicable to business-to-consumer (B2C) companies that manufacture purchasable goods, nor to larger firms with research capabilities. In fact, startups and small and medium-sized enterprises (SMEs) are more adept at rapid-fire strategies of finding an answer in the market through low-budget experiments, and there are examples that illustrate this rationale.

Taekyung Chemical태경 케미컬, based in Seosan, located on the western coast of the Korean peninsula, is a typical business-to-business (B2B) company that supplies dry ice to CJ Logistics and other delivery companies. It had the foresight to recognize the growth of online food purchases and made preparations in advance. The company injected a 2.5 billion won investment to set up automated manufacturing lines and develop dry ice specifically for food deliveries. It won contracts from fastidious retailers such as Coupang and Market Kurly. At the same time, it ran a "Safer, Fresher" branding campaign for its products. The company's determination paid off amidst booming untact businesses, reaching the top of the rapidly growing domestic dry ice market, and saw its stocks surge. This example shows that regardless of whether it's a B2B company, an SME, a government or an organization, the core competency in V-nomics is the ability to respond to change.

"The Plague was a turning point in the Middle Ages that led to the Renaissance," said Professor Yoo Hyunjoon of Hongik University. "If not for the Plague, we may have seen the Middle Ages drag on into the 20th century. COVID-19 may prove to be an opportunity for a true renaissance."[18]

What steps should we take to turn this crisis into an opportunity for a true renaissance and make sure that the world's sacrifices were not in vain? In the somber words of Klaus Schwab, founder and executive chairman of the World Economic Forum, "Adapt or die."

COWBOY HERO

OMNI-LAYERED HOMES

The home, typically considered a conventional and immovable space, is becoming an epicenter for change. In fact, "home and neighborhood" have been buzzwords for the past 10 years. The outbreak of COVID-19 in 2020 forced most people to stay at home, focusing their attention on the private domain. As a result, the home has shown its potential for transformation, adding myriads of new functions, much like the "layered look" in fashion, or the "layers" used in a Photoshop image.

There are three major layers to the modern home. The first is the Basic Layer, in which its traditional function as a place of rest and privacy has intensified. The second is the Additional Layer, one which allows us to accomplish tasks that were previously only completed outside the home. And lastly, the Expanding Layer interacts with the neighborhood, introducing functions that are not limited to the home but extend to the immediate surrounding area.

In the Basic Layer, the primary function of the home is enhanced, leading to advances in hygiene appliances, furniture and interior industries, and to upscale upgrades with hotel-quality goods or maintenance robots. In the Additional Layer, the home becomes a multifunctioning area for education, work, shopping, hobbies, exercise, and entertainment. And in the Expanding Layer, the concept of home is extended to its environs, broadening the scope of economic activity to within "slippers distance" of the home.

The pandemic has hurled us closer to the future. A "house," which had long been the object of desire as an asset that can be easily liquidated, has been redefined by its primary function as a "home" — a place of dwelling — showing its potential for even further transformation. The trend of the "Layered Home" indicates a paradigm shift, not just for Korea in 2021, but also for the future of the living space. The home will undoubtedly become the cradle for change in the future consumer industry.

The home has been the topic of an emerging trend among broadcasting circles. MBC's *Where is My Home*구해줘! 홈즈 took top ratings among viewers in the key 20-40 demographic for 31 straight weeks. EBS's *Home: An Architectural Journey*건축탐구-집 is another show in which architects introduce homes with their own unique charm. And viewers raved about *House on Wheels*바퀴 달린 집, which aired on tvN, as it portrayed the modern dilemma of wanting to travel in nature while still being at home.

Such "house programs" clearly illustrate the public's heightened interest in the home. In fact, "home and neighborhood" have been buzzwords for the past 10 years. Ever since our keyword phrase "Gotta be Cocooned" in the 2009 edition of this series, the topic has often reappeared throughout the series: "Into Our Neighborhood" (2010), "Playing in Hidden Alleys" (2015), "Hide Away in Your Querencia" (2018), "Emerging 'Millennial Family'" (2019) and "Immediate Satisfaction: the 'Last Fit Economy'" (2020). The outbreak of COVID-19 in 2020 forced most people to stay at home, seeing an explosion in their interest and involvement in the private domain. The home is being reimagined as a "multifunctional" space during the coronavirus era. The home has become a place where we eat, sleep, shop, play, study, work out, relax, create, and more. And astonishingly enough, tasks that seemed impossible to accomplish within this area are becoming all the more possible.

Our lifestyles may change along with the passage of time, and yet our home remains quite unchanged. When we get married and have kids, the hassle of packing up and moving to a bigger house becomes a natural part of life. However, as people sought refuge at home amid a viral outbreak that drove the world into a panic, the function of a house has become more flexible and multipurpose.

We would like to define this trend as the "Layered Home," indicative of how its functions have taken on multiple layers. First, the Basic Layer intensifies its traditional function as a place of rest and privacy. Second, the Additional Layer allows us to accomplish tasks during the outbreak that were previously done elsewhere. And lastly, the Expanding Layer interacts with the neighborhood, with its functions not limited to the home but extending to the immediate surrounding area. Let's look at each of these aspects of the Layered Home, which is slowly transforming from a simple and safe area into a multipurpose and all-embracing domain.

The Basic Layer: Enhancing the Basic Function of the Home

The groundwork for the Layered Home is the Basic Layer, which enhances its primary function as a refuge. The outbreak of COVID-19 has made it half-mandatory that people stay within their homes, enhancing and expanding their function as safe havens. Such adjustments have been a boon for hygiene-related home appliances, furniture and interior industries. First of all, consumer interest in hygiene and immunity naturally led to purchases of related home appliances. As the viral outbreak swept the nation from the end of January, sales of LG's Tromm Styler in February jumped 30 percent year-on-year, while those of SK's Magic Air Purifier for January-February rose 166 percent from a year earlier.[1] Sales of previously unpopular electronic goods such as disinfection gadgets and sterilizing lamps also jumped, as consumers tried to alleviate some of their anxiety about the outbreak by purchasing such products.

Home interior craze among stay-at-homes

Furniture sales marked the most obvious surge. Consumers previously favored experiential spending such as travel and "gastroventures." No longer possible during a pandemic, these expenditures are migrating to purchases of furniture. According to Statistics Korea, the home furnishing market

Bringing the hotel into the home. As they spend more time at home, more and more people are seeking to introduce a luxurious hotel-like ambience into their dwelling.

nearly doubled to 13.7 trillion won ($12.1 billion) in 2020 from 7 trillion won in 2008, and is expected to expand to 18 trillion won by 2023.[2] Home furniture, which was largely ignored due to the fact that it was always there, became all the more noticeable as people spent most of their time at home, naturally leading to an interest in remodeling and home interior design. Home furnishing manufacturers such as Hyundai Livart saw a 20 percent increase in revenue in the first half of 2020, while that of Hanssem 한샘 rose 19 percent and EMONS Furniture jumped 31 percent from a year earlier. Furniture trade on online shopping malls stood at 2.3 trillion won ($2 billion), with February seeing a 35 percent increase in revenue year on year. Sales of home study furnishing such as desks and bookcases jumped 42 percent, and that of living room furniture such as sofas reached a peak during the vacation period in July.[3]

Such trends are not limited to upgrading furniture, but also include redesigning a space more suitable to a user's taste. For example, the kitchen is no longer a domain exclusive to women, as millennials do not attach such labels to the communal area. Housing and building contractor Daelim대림산업 raised the height of their kitchen sinks following big data analysis that showed an increase in male participation in household chores. The younger generations also prefer to change the layout of their residential areas through remodeling. This is a marked change from the past when people were reluctant to change the layout of their houses because of fears of how it may affect real estate prices, or restoration concerns at the end of a lease contract. These days people are renovating and upgrading their homes to create a unique space of their own. As such, interior design platforms, which offer professional contractor services, are on the rise. "Today's House오늘의 집," an interior design information sharing platform, saw steady gains in the number of its users since its 2014 launch and recorded a spike in downloads in 2020, with its accumulated total exceeding 10 million by April 2020, up from 5 million a year earlier.[4]

I want to live in a hotel-like house

While the above changes stem from staying at home for a protracted period, others are seeking a luxurious upscale upgrade of their homes. A hotel-style, a gallery-style, or a resort-style home is what they want to achieve. These days, having a home that "looks like a hotel" is the pinnacle of compliments. Writer Kim Young-ha points out that "Spaces that have been lived in for a long period hold grievances," adding that the reason why we like going on vacations at hotels is because these spaces hold no day-to-day concerns for us.[5] People living in modern society, familiar with international travel and staying at hotels, want to recreate those experiences in their homes. Automated blinds and curtains, previously only seen in hotel rooms, can now be installed at a reasonable price. Advances in smart home technology has made possible audio controls for air-conditioning, lighting and curtains, all of which will be standard installations in homes designed by Hyundai E&C and Daewoo E&C. Remote control, state-of-the-art security, luxury bedding, unique fragrances and other elements that seemed exclusive to hotels are now finding their way into private homes.

Paintings are another indicator of home upscaling. Art rental businesses such as Open Gallery오픈갤러리, BlueCanvas 블루캔버스 and Gallery K갤러리K are seeing an uptick in orders. Open Gallery, which offers a subscription service in which users can pick new artwork every three months, saw subscriptions jump 71 percent in the first half of 2020 compared with a year earlier.[6] As paintings provide a finishing touch to interior decoration, artwork rental services will likely expand in the near future.

It's only natural to want to show off a completed interior design. Online housewarming parties are an emerging trend among single households. Homeowners upload pictures of the fruits of their labor on social media and invite friends to an online housewarming party. The journey begins by browsing through beautiful homes online, perhaps reading up on the stories behind their transformation, purchasing related items and then taking pictures of these items placed in their own homes. Online housewarming parties have become a popular segment on variety television shows, and similar videos are uploaded constantly on YouTube and Instagram.

The Additional Layer: Adding New Functions to the Home

The practical use of the home is becoming even more important as it takes on multifunctioning roles on top of its Basic Layer, such as office, classroom and holiday resort. In fact, most activities can be accomplished these days with a swipe of the finger on a smartphone. With advances in digital technology, the home has emerged as a versatile venue from where one can work, shop, enjoy oneself, work out, relax and do all kinds of daily activities.

Watching a concert and shopping on the living room sofa

The most significant change is that we can now enjoy concerts, performances and fashion shows from the comfort of our own living room. Virtual and livestream concerts have become a common parlance, with BTS's *Bang Bang Con*방방콘, held at the height of the pandemic, regarded as an event that was ahead of its time. The home can now transform into a concert stage, or a shopping mall. Online live commerce broadcasts, in which show hosts and shoppers can communicate and exchange ideas, are breaking down barriers in home shopping.

Giant corporations such as Naver, CJ Olive Young, GS Home Shopping and Shinsegae TV Shopping, have all jumped into the live commerce market. Goods available on live commerce have also become varied, showcasing fashion, beauty and food products, widening the scope for consumers. As retailers desperately seek sales channels that were limited by the pandemic and social distancing measures, and jump to online platforms, shoppers are now able to access a wider variety of goods such as duty-free items that could only be bought at duty-free stores. Even car dealers are introducing live commerce platforms. In September 2020, Hyundai Motors launched Channel Hyundai, an interactive application for smart TVs to livestream events such as the unveiling of new models, or provide 3D renderings of its cars that shoppers can examine in detail as if visiting a showroom. Furthermore, the company is operating its Hyundai Showroom Live, an online showroom service that offers one-on-one video conferencing between dealers and overseas clients and plans to expand the service worldwide.

The home becomes a fitness center

Fitness buffs were forced to find ways to work out from home due to the pandemic and subsequent announcement of social distancing measures that shut down most public facilities, including gyms and fitness centers. The rising demand for home fitness caused a surge in the sales of related products. According to CJ Logistics' "Daily Life Report Plus," which analyzed delivery items for March-April 2020, home fitness products related to yoga and Pilates jumped 128 percent, treadmills surged 266 percent, steppers rose 162 percent, and free weights and dumbbells climbed 140 percent from a year earlier. SSG.com also reported a 42 percent year-on-year rise in home fitness products for February-June 2020.[7]

Social distancing prompted many people stuck at home to create their own fitness rooms. According to a survey of 1,000 people by Macromill Embrain on "Korean perceptions of healthy life and exercise," nine in ten people (92.3%) replied that they exercise, 44.5 percent replied that they work out at home, 28 percent chose the park and 19.6 percent trained in the gym. Home fitness, which had been previously limited to following movements and routines on YouTube videos, has become a wide-open market.[8] Advances in motion detection technology and AI coaching systems

Working and working out from home. The home has become a hub of daily activity where anything is possible.

have allowed users to work out anywhere and at any time.

More people are finding it easier to enjoy exercising with the aid of a mobile app, following instructors whenever and wherever they wish. Peloton, sometimes dubbed the "Tesla of fitness," raised its valuation $1.16 billion on its September 2019 IPO, and its 12-month retention rate reached a whopping 93 percent. Its business model, which couples exercise bikes with monthly subscriptions to online video training sessions, is the reason why the company also earned its recent nickname "the Netflix of exercise," churning out many fitness addicts. Content is key to Peloton's success. Monthly fees allows users to attend online sessions and buying the related equipment allows users to work out from home. They can even join others in a studio setting. The ability to work out, free from restraints of time, place or weather, along with other users of similar fitness levels, has helped the company create value through this business model.

Everything is now possible at home

The pandemic has also changed the way we entertain ourselves. YouTube is overflowing with content for having fun at home, and over-the-top media services such as Netflix have seen a surge in users. People have turned isolation into a new form of enjoyment. YouTubers are uploading videos on various ways to pass the time during quarantine and have also recorded vlogs about quarantine life. Generation MZ's remarkable capacity to adapt gave birth to "voluntary labor-intensive" recipes such as Dalgona달고나 coffee soufflés that require 1,000 whisks, or Jetty제티 chocolate rice cake made by stirring its mixture 400 times.

Console games, which had been losing their market share to mobile games, found favor with gamers again as they were forced to stay indoors. Console games require bulky consoles such as the Xbox or PlayStation to be hooked up to

TVs, which is one of the factors that led gamers to begin the transition to mobile games that can be enjoyed anywhere and at any time. However, the advantages of console gaming have reemerged as a beacon of light to relieve some gamers' frustration with being stuck at home, where games can be enjoyed on a large screen with the whole family. Game developers such as NCSoft, Netmarble, and Nexon, which traditionally focused on making PC and mobile games, are also showing interest in developing console games. Nintendo's Ring Fit Adventure, a successor to Wii Fit, was sold out due to the popularity of at-home fitness routines, as it combines elements of the action role-playing genre with exercise.

Self-isolation also disrupted styling and beauty routines. The lack of visits to hair salons, barber shops and esthetic clinics resulted in unkempt hairdos and graying roots. People have become masters of self-styling and self-beauty routines, dying their own roots and taking care of their own skin with relevant home beauty care products. In the coronavirus era, the beauty industry has entered modern homes. According to a study by LG Economic Research Institute, the market for beauty appliances is showing an annual growth of 10 percent and its market size is expected to reach 1.6 trillion won ($1.4 billion) by 2022.[9]

Home beauty is a prime example of an aspect of the Additional Layer. In 2020, purchases of beauty products shot up as people needed to soothe their skin after continuous friction from wearing masks. In line with this frenzy for home esthetic goods, previously unfamiliar LED facial masks are making inroads in the market through a variety of experiential events. Advances in beauty technology allowed InBody인바디 machines, which measure body fat composition, to be used in the home, while neck wrinkle smoothers, leg massagers, EMS (electrical muscle stimulation) low frequency massagers and other beauty-related appliances are quickly taking the market by storm. Devices that were only previously available at esthetic clinics and beauty shops are becoming smaller and cheaper, allowing users to enjoy expert skincare routines at home.

The Expanding Layer: The Home and the Neighborhood

The proximity between one's workplace and home used to be a major factor to determine the quality of life of office workers. However, as teleworking became the new normal, our homes became our workplace. The home has transformed from a place where people rest their weary bodies after work to a place where people work and even socialize. And as the home becomes the center of our daily lives, the commercial area in its immediate vicinity — within "slippers distance" of the home — has emerged. Nearby facilities make up for what's lacking in the home. It extends the concept of "home" to the immediate neighborhood, becoming part of the Expanding Layer.

Offline mom and pop stores that have been struggling against the onslaught of e-commerce have embraced the "slippers distance" concept, appealing to neighborhood regulars with their friendliness, familiarity, trustworthiness and secureness. Convenience stores such as CU and GS25 are implementing walking-distance deliveries: regular customers can order products from nearby stores delivered swiftly by staff members, who are also likely to be neighbors. Traffic congestion is not an issue due to their proximity. The "slippers distance" concept encompasses infinite possibilities and has opened a new chapter in online-to-offline services. Some have even taken to calling their nearby convenience stores "our home refrigerator." Eliminating the fridge from their homes helps open up much of their kitchen space. This concept, that renders the refrigerator unnecessary at home, is indicative of how flexible people have become in reimagining their place of dwelling.

The home can also be a place where one's tastes and sensibilities meet with those of others. The website "Naamezip Project" 남의 집 프로젝트("남의 집" means "another's house"), introduced the concept of "trips to living rooms," in which homeowners turn their living areas into open salons and host events for strangers who share common hobbies, interests and knowledge. Members can browse through various get-togethers in different settings such as a living room decorated with Buddhist artwork, a parlor that looks like an Italian fresco, or a vegetable garden filled with organic produce. These gatherings that bring together four to six people with common interests into the hosts' living room cost between 20,000 won and 50,000 won ($17-$44) per person and last about three to four hours. The service, which was launched in 2017, has organized 700-odd gatherings hosted by about 500 homeowners, attracting some 3,500 participants.[10] These "trips to living rooms" have opened the door to a new form of leisure and cultural activity that allows people to share their interests and philosophy in the private setting of their own homes.

Background: Rediscovery of Remote Living

Changes in social mood and thinking among society's members lead to the transformation of a space's use and classification. The 2020 viral outbreak was a massive turning point that shook social norms and paradigms. If we take a look at the rationale behind the multiple layers of the home, we can first point out changes in consumers' perceptions who now benefit from no longer wasting time moving from one place to another. According to a 2019 survey of daily schedules by Statistics Korea, the average office worker used to spend an hour and 16 minutes commuting every day; over an hour of precious time was wasted on the road.[11] That is why the issue of proximity between the workplace and home was such a hot topic. And when they suddenly shifted to teleworking, they realized just how much time they had spent commuting on the road. That they could stay at home, complete their tasks and still get paid became an appealing prospect.

An increasing number of companies are adopting flexible working policies such as teleworking to minimize the spread of COVID-19, with some even giving employees the freedom to choose the time and place to work. According to a survey of the nation's top 500 companies by revenue, regarding their working policies following the viral outbreak, 75 percent had adopted flexible working systems, and a majority (51.1%) of them will likely maintain the new policy even after the pandemic subsides.[12]

In addition to this perspectival shift in remote working, people have also come to realize the value of "remote living," in which they distance themselves from others and experience various services during the period of forced (or self-imposed) isolation. Consumers, who have realized that there are in fact advantages to managing their daily tasks and activities from home, and that it wasn't as bad as they had feared, are trying to create their own layers. They can be informed of world news, even exercise, shop and participate in communal activities in the comfort of their own homes, as advances in technology enrich their stuck-at-home lives.

DIY buffs specializing in broadcasting, beauty, leisure and interior design, also contributed to changes in consumer trends. Instead of calling on experts or professionals, people are now more familiar with watching, learning from and following tutorials on YouTube and television to accomplish various tasks. Not only do they challenge themselves by following such tutorials, they also upload videos and pictures of the results on social media, sharing the experience with friends. The stay-at-homes of today are learning about finding joy and entertainment even before noticing any inconvenience from confinement.

Outlook and Implications

— Home: The cradle for the future consumer industry

"The home of the future will be more than just a house and will have everything a person wants."

These are the words of futurist Thomas Frey, executive director of the Colorado-based DaVinci Institute. Ironically, COVID-19 has brought us closer to the future of space. We experimented with infinite possibilities as we re-examined the purpose of the home and realized its value as a manifestation of our happiness, rather than just a piece of real estate to be bought and sold. An area affects the way people think. Open areas are conducive to creativity, and free movement fosters a positive mindset. The house of the future will likely become versatile to enable all such activities. The home is a living entity that responds to the needs of its inhabitants and can improve upon itself, depending on the implemented ideas and customized technology.

People who have previously emphasized the economic value of homes are now realizing a need to re-examine its significance and changes to its functionality stemming from spiritual and philosophical values. The Layered Home is the trend of perceiving the living space as an area to create one's lifestyle that also reflects the inhabitant's future-oriented attitude towards life. The trend of the Layered Home also implies that members of the household need to readjust their relationships with one another. Rather than an unchanging layout that divides space into the main bedroom, children's room and living room, the home needs to become more flexible to ensure both personal and communal hours, to allow for personal and individual tastes to be expressed as well as for shared family time. The Layered Home can take on multiple layers: a room that reflects the dweller's preferences; a room fitted with informational technology for teleworking and homeschooling; a living room with furniture that can be transformed depending on the time of day; or a house that can change its interior layout according to one's work or hobbies.

Such transformations require the necessary changes in

policy. The Ministry of Land, Infrastructure and Transport is working toward a more versatile housing supply policy that reflects the high possibility of homes becoming places of work, learning and other activities in the future. Its plans for long-life housing, in which homes will be built for durability to last a century, will incorporate pillar-like structures for support rather than relying on load-bearing walls, allowing for more flexible variation of a house's layout, more interchangeable spaces, and even a reduction in noise complaints. For example, Daelim's proposal for its C2 (Creative Living + Customizing Space) houses eliminates interior walls and allows for flexible layout transformations in line with their concept of a creative space that reflects individual dispositions and personality. This implies that future apartments within the same complex will no longer have cookie cutter layouts.

And lastly, the trend of the Layered Home has implications for the infinite possibilities of advances in technology that support an "untact" environment. Digital transformation will rapidly take over not only businesses but also the daily lives of consumers. Home automation technology has yet to become a household standard. There have been many technological attempts, such as "ubiquitous" tech of the early 2000s, smart homes of the 2010s, and the recent spotlight on IoT (Internet of things) homes, but the home remains a relatively conservative domain. It will be interesting to see whether electronic appliance makers will be able to make inroads with such technology in an age heavily focused on the home. According to French philosopher Gaston Bachelard:

"Our house is our corner of the world. As has often been said, it is our first universe, a real cosmos in every sense of the world."

— from *La Poétique de l'Espace* (The Poetics of Space) (1958)

It may be somewhat of a cliché, but the home is the basis of our livelihood, and the foundation for our very existence. It no longer remains simply a private space but comes together with other individual homes to create a dwelling culture that represents a society and an era. The trend of the Layered Home is a paradigm shift that points the way to the future of residential space. Spatial transformations will lead to changes in the way we think. When minds change, so does the future. The home will undoubtedly become the cradle for change in the future consumer industry.

WE ARE THE MONEY-FRIENDLY GENERATION

A generation familiar with the components of capitalism such as ads, markets and financing, and conversant with the very nature of capitalism, has emerged as key players among today's consumers. The "Money-friendly Generation" share the same traits as the "World Cup Generation" who grew up aspiring to become professional soccer players watching the 2002 World Cup. This does not mean that the Money-friendly Generation can only be found among the younger generations. Older generations are no stranger to the principle of capitalism since the IMF bailed out the nation during its 1997 financial crisis, which changed their perception of the economy and of consumption. At the end of the day, a member of the Money-friendly Generation is anyone who is well-versed in the language of capitalism.

This group has an appreciation for market profits and as such is tolerant and makes use of advertising. They are honest about their desires and unhesitating in their pursuit of happiness through their spending. They put effort into the process and are never wasteful. Even when "flexing," or strutting their spending power, they sort out what to buy and what to rent, and observe reasonable spending habits in their own way by comparing prices and numerous purchase channels. They are also keen on investing. Couples who often sit in cafés chatting about recent movie releases are changing their typical dating venues to attend open houses in search for a potential real estate investment. Soldiers and university students are also getting in on the act. Amid an influx of economic and market information, this generation becomes human capital and jumps into the competitive fray, suffering from economic uncertainties, yet refraining from becoming materialistic or overly impulsive. They are impulsive, however, in their pursuit of happiness, and are meticulous planners of their future. Armed with a new concept of the economy, they will emerge as leaders of V-nomics, and beyond.

"Please turn on ads and allow embedding in your videos. You've put so much effort into them."

– A comment on the YouTube channel *Chasan's Common Legal Knowledge*

"I hear embedded ads will increase YouTube algorithm exposure. Please turn on ads so more people know about your content!"

– A comment on YouTube channel *DanoTV*

YouTube channels that provide rewarding information and forgo ads, affectionately dubbed "benevolent" channels, often attract such comments. The older generations, who invariably click on "Skip Ad," are usually taken aback by such requests. But it is only natural for today's consumers, who learned at a young age that "every purchase requires payment," to accept ads as a part of subscribing to the content. Watching an ad is akin to showing affection as a fan, with the knowledge that it generates income for the YouTuber. The reference to YouTube's algorithm also demonstrates the viewer's notable familiarity with how income is generated in the process.

This not only indicates changes in the perception of advertising; a growing segment of the younger generations are weary of conventions about money and spending. Luxury brands no longer represent the shameless face of capitalism, but rather represent an assertive preference best described by the new expression: "my money, my purchase." The definition of personal savings is transformed into, say, a six-month installment plan to save up for a trip that's sure to bring happiness. This does not mean that the younger generations only know about how to·spend money. They no longer frown upon money-grubbing, but rather take time to research and become more versed in investments and the flow of money with a clear understanding that it will greatly benefit them.

An upcoming generation that grew up watching or experiencing an iconic event usually gets dubbed as the "________ Generation." The "Pak Seri박세리 Generation" are a group of young ladies that took to the greens watching the historic LPGA win by the legendary golfer. The "World Cup Generation" are soccer players who aspired to join the national team, playing in the K-League at home or even in La Liga or the English Premier League. The "Money-friendly Generation" is what we can call these consumers who have become attuned to the very nature of capitalism and optimized for its economic activity, by growing up, learning, eating, and playing according to its set of rules.

The word "capitalism" may seem quite weighty. However, in Korean society today, it has come to represent market principles to a larger extent and is often used in witty commentary on current social conditions. A "capitalistic smile" is used to describe a pretentious gesture that seeks profit. If an idol singer stars in a coffee ad, despite his distaste for the beverage, it will be joked that so-and-so "bowed down before mighty capitalism." The term "Money-friendly Generation" (which was literally "Capitalist Kids자본주의 키즈" in the original Korean edition of this book) is neither weighty nor trivial commentary on today's consumers who merely possess a different sense of reality and economic concepts from that of the past.

The Money-friendly Generation are not necessarily limited to the younger generations. Some members of the old guard share a similar view with the younger generations as they are no stranger to the principle of capitalism since the IMF bailout in 1997. In other words, Money-freindly Generation can refer to those who are well-versed in the language of capitalism. They were brand consumers from birth and consider the pursuit of profit a base instinct – a departure from the mindset and way of living in the past. Let's take a closer look at the Money-friendly Generation, the darlings of the market economy, who exhibit a unique approach to the value and nature of money.

The Rise of the Money-friendly Generation

As key players of change in the market, the Money-friendly Generation consumers show a markedly different attitude compared with past generations. These changes are notable especially in (1) "Advertising," which attests to their understanding and practical utilization of the market; (2) "Spending," the most visible indicator of their preferences; and (3) "Managing Finances," a vital part of their economic activity. Let's take an in-depth look at how the Money-friendly Generation stands out.

1. Advertising: One promotional word makes up for a thousand subscriptions

Yoo Jae-suk: A music video these days costs 3 million won ($2,500).
Rain: That's a pittance.
Yoo Jae-suk: My Yoo San-seul music video cost just 2.5 million!
Lee Hyori: Shall I get us some sponsors? We can each use or wear one thing, as a promotion. And you <hands a bag of snacks to Rain> *can start by munching on these.*

So went a frank discussion about product placement during an episode of *Hangout with Yoo*놀면 뭐하니?, a weekend reality show on MBC. Not only were they candid about the production costs for their upcoming music video, they disclosed plans to land promotions to fund their project.

The episode even showed the stars eating and drinking these products, with subtitles such as, "Are you watching, dear sponsors?" making it clear they were embedded intentionally. The response was largely positive with many viewers commenting that they had "never seen such adorable product placement."

Embedded products, especially in reality and variety programs, had up until recently remained low-key (with the goods literally placed on tables where they can be fleetingly shown in scenes) due to concerns that they interrupted viewer immersion. The use of product placement as a comedic element signals a change in consumer attitudes. Viewers understand that broadcasters need to attract sponsors to fund their programs and readily give a pass when the camera pans to a product or logo. In fact, they voice their appreciation when producers manage to subtly incorporate the products in their programs. Such trends have even spawned a show dedicated entirely to embedded products. *If It Was on Television*텔레비전에 그게 나왔으면, launched in July 2020 on SBS, makes use of broadcasting regulations that state that products can be shown but not discussed, and turns it into a game. And because it features products made by SMEs (small and medium-sized enterprises), the overall response has been positive. The Nonsan strawberries featured during its pilot episode in April became sold out, and other products on the show grabbed top spots on a list of trending internet searches.

Online content, which fosters closer relations between producers and viewers, uses advertisements more readily. As mentioned in the introduction, YouTube videos are filled with comments such as "I didn't skip the ads," or "I won't click the 'Skip Ad' button in hopes that you earn more and keep creating good content." When YouTubers insert ads toward the end of their videos in consideration of their viewers, fans ask them in the comment section to place ads in the middle of their clips.

This is how the Money-friendly Generation, as subscribers, show their affection, accepting such subscription "costs" as the new "merchandise" they engage with. Viewers support their favorite YouTuber by helping out with their "homework." When a YouTuber is asked to upload a review or a video of them using a sponsored product, it's colloquially known as "doing homework." The sponsoring company usually appraises the advertising impact through the comments attached to the video, and therefore viewers will leave comments such as, "I saw the ad," or leave comments obviously aimed at pleasing the sponsors, cheekily adding, "This is how we should leave comments, right? (wink wink)." It has even become an entertainment factor for the viewer. Some congratulate lesser-known YouTubers when they start uploading sponsored content, giving them a pat on the back saying, "My, how the channel has grown," which shows how viewers clearly understand the market principles at work.

Some consumers have stepped beyond passively ingesting a company's advertising, choosing rather to actively induce them. Some may feel that pop-up ads on Instagram and other social media feeds are invasive, especially when such ads are linked to their recent internet searches. However, the Money-friendly Generation considers these ads as just another bit of informative content that can help reduce the need for repeated internet searches. One often feels lost amid an oversupply of information, losing track of where to even begin a new search. With multiple keyword searches, users may discover unheard of brands and products while swiping through their social media accounts, tapping on embedded links that allow for easy access and purchases.

2. Spending: "Irrational spending" doesn't exist in my dictionary

"Proofies" of luxury items and their clearly visible logo-emblazoned boxes, or of a wad of cash splayed out as evidence of one's hard-earned pay, are part of the emerging "flex" trend. Those who are used to more subtle displays as a measure of wealth or bragging rights are naturally taken aback by such outright ostentation. What is the reason for the craze? "Flex" is defined as the act of curving or bending, and

They are nonchalant about outlandish displays of wealth. To them, reproaching it as vulgar is outdated. Give the devil his due, is their motto.

is of course commonly used to describe the act of contracting one's muscles in a boasting display of muscular strength and physique. African American rappers who exemplify a rags-to-riches story began using the term in the 1990s to show off their wealth and success, and it is this meaning that underlies its current usage.[1] In other words, "flex" is not a stunt undertaken by those born with a silver spoon, but is rather a desire to seek recognition for one's success achieved through hard work. What is noteworthy is the attitude of the Money-friendly Generation in this regard. They do not dismiss such actions as a vulgar display of wealth but accept it as the right of the worthy. They recognize the ability to spend money on whatever they want as an inherent feature of capitalism and don't feel the need to hide their envy of such displays.

The Money-friendly Generation transcends the cool-headed response to advertising, and its members are frank in their consumerist desires, the driving force of a market economy. They feel a sense of accomplishment in attaining that which is not easily obtainable and acknowledge that expressing oneself through discerned spending is a basic form of the pursuit of happiness that is true to capitalistic instincts. There is no such thing as being too young to consume something. Musinsa무신사, a popular shopping platform among teenagers and those in their 20s, features more than 1,400 luxury brand products on their website (as of August 2020). Customers 18 years or younger were responsible for 48 percent of the monthly 1,200-count search for a 190,000 won ($160) brand-name T-shirt. Some 37 percent of the 80,000-odd buyers of foreign cars in Korea in the first half of 2020 were those in their teens, 20s and 30s.[2] The Money-friendly Generation asserts that the brand purchases are not to simply gain acceptance among peers but are a means of expressing one's individuality.

When allowing for the level of income of the younger generations, such spending on luxury brands may seem extravagant, but the spending pattern is in fact within their means. They carefully investigate which luxury brands and goods are good value for money. The value of the purchase lies not just in practical efficiency, but also in its symbolic value. Once a target is set, they will likely compare available discounts and promotions to save just a few thousand won even when the price tag is in the range of a few million won.

Prior generations may have felt the need to visit a department store to buy luxury goods, but this new breed of customers compare prices online and sometimes opt for rentals, depending on the period of use. According to online rental shops, customers prefer an outright purchase of steady sellers such as Chanel products, but choose rental options for goods that have a limited fashion cycle. The purchase strategy is reasonable in its own way because rentals allow them to obtain a product while it is still fashionable at a fraction of the retail cost. They may also choose to buy high-end products depending on the resellability of a brand.

The Money-friendly Generation, who are well-versed in active spending, also enjoy the process as if they are taking part in a game. "Drops" and "raffles," emerging as the latest trends in marketing, are the game versions of spending, adding an element of entertainment to product-related events where the chance of actually succeeding to purchase an item is next to nil. A "drop" is when a seller unexpectedly releases a limited-edition item. A typical example is Musinsa's online drop of Chamisul참이슬 (a traditional soju brand) backpacks in 2019, which sold out within 5 minutes and had potential buyers setting their alarms for the drop time in a fierce competition. A successful purchase grants the buyer a breathtaking thrill, as well as a 49,000 won ($43) product that has a potential resale value of three to four times the original price, resulting in a tidy sum for the lucky few.[3] The frenzy surrounding the drop led to adverse side-effects, such as part-time surrogate queuers who were paid to stand in line for others.

To address concerns of unfairness, and to meet a strong sense of justice, "raffle marketing" emerged as an alternative to the drop. This is when the seller hands out lotteries online or offline within a limited time frame and then sells the product to the raffle holder. Musinsa's two-day raffle for 500 Pengsoo펭수 T-shirts in December 2019 drew a crowd of 25,000. Such notoriety prompted some retailers to set a "dress code" for those lining up. For the November 2019 release of the "Para Noise" edition of Air Force 1 sneakers, Nike required those lining up for the raffle to don a Nike T-shirt and Air Force 1s, giving loyal customers the opportunity to show their zeal for Nike. Drops and raffles are a new spending approach for the Money-friendly Generation who spare no effort in obtaining rarities and seeking novel experiences.

3. Managing Finances: Investment fever among young people

Investment has become a hot topic in recent years at gatherings for those in their 20s and 30s, regardless of gender or profession. Young people, whose major interests used to be movies or TV programs, are more readily chatting about investment opportunities. It is no longer rare to see couples attending lectures on real estate investment and going to a property's open house while on a date.

Among university students, investment study clubs, real estate research, value investments, and proptech (property technology) are all the rage. A middle school student wrote on an online investment community board that while his peers play mobile and computer games, he would rather buy stocks in a game company, such as Netmarble or Nexon. And as the military permitted the use of smartphones on bases, a new tribe of individual investors (referred to as "ants" in Korea) has emerged, calling themselves "soldier ants."

More and more young people are turning to investment financing for quick returns rather than letting funds lie idle. As a group that grew up well provided for, worrying about money is a given for the Money-friendly Generation to steer clear of any future misfortune. Managing one's finances begins with savings. "Spare-change finance잔돈금융" is an introduction to managing one's money and allows the hard-up newbie to make a habit of saving money. KakaoBank's Piggy

Bank service automatically saves any amount less than 1,000 won in their accounts, the savings balance of which is shown with images of items of equivalent value, such as a bowl of *jjajangmyun*짜장면 or a Seoul-Busan KTX train ticket, letting the user feel the power of saving money. It was so popular that it had a million accounts within 13 days of its launch.[4] Kookmin Bank's "KB Smart StarPhone Savings" app enables the user to feel the satisfaction of saving money by forgoing small niceties. For example, if you decide to skip your morning coffee, you press a coffee icon on your phone which transfers that amount to your savings account. Shinhan Card teamed up with Shinhan Investment to offer fractional trading on overseas blue chips such as Amazon, Apple, Nike and Starbucks, in units of one-hundredth (0.01) of a stock. Its customers can feel the satisfaction of becoming (micro) shareholders of global giants with a small investment. The key to spare-change finance is the element of amusement that younger generations can enjoy to satiate their thirst for investment with just a small amount of money.

The Money-friendly Generation makes an effort to learn the ropes step by step, with a clear understanding that they are responsible for managing their own funds. They watch videos on YouTube about economic history and liberal arts, study up on the basics of the stock trading software Home Trading System (HTS) and conduct mock investments by watching livestreams of stock charts. Joining study

The ultimate dream for the Money-friendly Generation is to earn as much money and as quickly as possible, become independent, and go into early retirement, in other words, become a member of the FIRE Tribe.

groups and open chat rooms with supplementary lessons help answer questions and share know-how on investment techniques. Stock investment garnered considerable interest during the pandemic, but YouTube channels offering investment tips have long been a staple for those in their 20s and 30s for the past two to three years.

The Money-friendly Generation's investments in various areas can be widely observed. With total gold investments expected to surpass 1 trillion won ($875 billion) since its launch, it is evident that younger generations are increasingly interested in investing, with 38 percent of accounts listed with the KRX gold market belonging to those in their 30s,

29 percent to those in their 40s, and 18 percent to those in their 20s.[5] They also dare to invest in real estate, previously regarded as an investment exclusive to the older generations. According to the Korea Appraisal Board's statistics on real estate trading, 28.8 percent of apartments purchased in the Seoul area in 2019 (20,691 out of 71,734) were made by those in their 30s. That same age bracket accounted for 32.4 percent in June 2020, followed by those in their 40s with 27.8 percent, further widening the gap. Because of a lack of funds, those in their 20s and 30s often venture into real estate investment through auctions or peer to peer (P2P) real estate funding.

According to P2P real estate investment platform HonestFund, investors in their 30s made up 36 percent of the total, while those in their 20s took a 31 percent share in April 2020. Given that those in their 20s took a 9 percent share in 2018, we can see a rapid downward trend in the average age of real estate investors.[6]

To be sure, the recent fever over real estate investment also lies in record-low interest rates, an all-time high in excess liquidity, and changing real estate regulations. Still, changes in the Money-friendly Generation's financial views were undoubtedly a key driving factor.

The Money-friendly Generation firmly believes that the sooner one starts managing finances, the better, laying out plans for and beyond retirement. Planning for one's retirement was previously viewed as equivalent to planning for old age, a key concern for the middle-aged and older. But for the Money-friendly Generation such concerns begin from the moment they join the workforce. This is represented in the arrival of the "FIRE (Financial Independence, Retire Early) Tribe": those who aspire to an ASAP retirement. This new group cuts all spending, except for barebone necessities, pouring up to 70 percent of their income into savings and then retiring around 40, or even younger. They then live off the returns on their investments, enjoying the lives they had always wished for, whether it be in leisure or volunteering. On the surface, the Money-friendly Generation and the Fire Tribe may seem at odds but ultimately, they share the same goal: economic freedom unfettered by monetary concerns. They simply take different paths to arrive at the same goal.

Background : Information Overload Stemming from Economic Instability

The Money-friendly Generation ponders over the life it wishes to lead, how much that would require and how to plan shrewdly to make it a reality. Its members have become rational creatures of desire, largely due to growing up in a society of digital information. Prior generations learned the ABCs of spending and finance management by observing spending patterns of their parents, or through daily experience in society. Nowadays, information is readily available anytime, anywhere, for anyone, regardless of age, and varies widely in quality and quantity.

YouTube provides answers to questions that you wouldn't even know how to ask your closest friends, including the annual income of a person working in a particular field, or tips and experience from billionaires on how to manage one's money. Communities on social media share the smallest bits of information in real time, including detailed receipts. The evolution of information technology has broken down behavioral patterns. One can purchase overseas stocks with a few swipes on a phone regardless of differing time zones, and, with advances in platform services, even offer a luxury handbag as a present through a messaging app. However, one cannot simply attribute this "capitalist sensibility" to changes in their behavioral patterns stemming from information overload. Let's take a look at the Money-friendly Generation's background to better understand them.

A generation of capital, by capital, and for capital

The emotions and sensibility of the Money-friendly Generation were nurtured in today's environment as well as in childhood within "the framework of capitalism."

American journalist Malcolm Harris wrote in his 2017 book, *Kids These Days*, that millennials were shaped through their perception as human capital. This theory turns humans into an economic concept, regarding them as a form of capital, requiring them to boost efficiency through attaining higher levels of education and training, and throwing them into fierce competition for higher income to prove their worth as excellent human capital.

This is a familiar story in South Korea. Children grow accustomed to being assessed through test scores and learn about the importance of capital through private lessons. As a result, this generation prioritizes the economic value of a life over the diverse possibilities of a life. As human capital, growing up in the framework of capitalism, economic instability further underlined the importance of capital. The IMF bailout, as well as the financial crisis triggered in the U.S. in 2007, were lessons in insecurity. The high unemployment rates of today have added to the instability. Their vulnerability will likely increase in the future amid a precarious job market. The all-too-apparent socioeconomic differences only fuel their desire for money. Daily comparisons of affluence on social media aside, a running joke goes that "in order to buy a house in Seoul, one should start saving from the days of King Geunchogo (AD 346-375)." Such is the reality of socioeconomic polarization in Korea. As a generation that has only experienced a society under capitalism, its members can only hope to plow through such adversity by becoming the most proficient in capitalism's rules and thereby emerging victorious.

Impulsive pursuit of happiness and meticulous planning: a dual view of time

The Money-friendly Generation's innate insecurity does not mean that their minds are only filled with worry. Anxiety about the future has given them, paradoxically, the power to focus on the present. While preparing methodically for the future, they never miss out on opportunities to enjoy the experiences of today. In other words, the *carpe diem* spirit denoted by the phrase "You only live once (YOLO)" does not necessarily mean that you have to give up on your future. A person with meticulous financial planning may spend a considerable amount to make a once-in-a-lifetime acquisition of a limited-edition item. Today's savings and debts are certainly closely linked to future resources. Splurging today means less funds for tomorrow. This is why the Money-friendly Generation makes use of multiple accounts. While they automatically set aside part of their income as savings for tomorrow, they enjoy a portion to satisfy their need for a "small but certain happiness"소확행. This could be an actual account, or a psychological one, with which they seek to satisfy an emotional need through flexible use. They may want to save up for a trip, settling with instant noodles from a convenience store for lunch; or they may want to save up for a major purchase of their favorite luxury brand, setting aside their usual preoccupation with cost efficiency.

Meticulous financial management by the Money-friendly

Generation is their way of enjoying a YOLO-inspired, small but certain happiness every now and then, all the while dealing with a sense of insecurity for the future.

Outlook and Implications

— Consumers who plan their lives with a balanced perspective

Teenage students these days often attach #sponsorswelcome 협찬환영 tags on their social media accounts. These ordinary students, who are by no means power bloggers or influencers, offer their services to advertise products. These teenagers seeking to earn some pocket money are well aware that companies like to make use of reviews from the general public and contact micro influencers who can generate word-of-mouth buzz at a low cost. The phenomenon, which is in accordance with the traits of the Money-friendly Generation, overlaps with examples given by Harvard University professor Michael Sandel in his 2012 book, *What Money Can't Buy: The Moral Limits of Markets.* An international airline company offered $777 to those willing to shave the back of their heads and stick on temporary tattoos as part of a marketing campaign. Another restaurant offered free lunches for life for anyone willing to get a permanent body tattoo of the eatery's logo. It meant that people can turn their bodies into a billboard for a nominal fee. Is it a stretch of the imagination to think that the Money-friendly Generation would take up such propositions?

Some may think, "What's the problem, if it's paid for?" Market principles can turn anything into an object of transaction. However, Sandel warns of the dangers of such "marketism." For example, if we start putting a price tag on friendliness, then the smile of a store clerk becomes not a show of kindness towards the customer but a right that the buyer deserves as payment for services rendered. The store clerk too will consider it a part of one's duty that need not be provided without financial remuneration, and the value on good among men and women will decline.

We need to take a hard look at whether the increase in the number of the Money-friendly Generation represents a natural part of capitalist society, or if it indicates that values which "money can't buy" are being brushed to the side.

There are some concerns that society may be headed in the wrong direction. The term "capitalism-born monsters자낳괴" best illustrates these concerns. It was used to describe how some online live streamers used to undertake preposterous stunts to earn "donations" or cyber money from viewers. The word "monster" shows the inherent concern about such incidents, but also raises the question of whether or not our society breeds such monsters.

And what of the companies? How should they cater to the market-savvy Money-friendly Generation? A recent uproar over furtive advertising was a hard lesson for corporate marketing practices. Content claiming to be impartial reviews in the vein of "my money, my purchase" turned out to have received corporate sponsorship. A slew of influencers issued formal apologies and announced they would halt all online activities. The Money-friendly Generation has a strong sense of identity and is clear about how it wants to spend its time and money. Its members select which advertisements to watch according to their own values and makes their own investments rather than entrusting it to a third party. Companies need to communicate clearly with such customers to earn their trust by respecting them, similar to how up-front product placement has gained a following.

A generation that also embraces anti-capitalist views

Companies also need to contemplate the value it wishes to impart on its customers, beyond seeking wider profit margins. Oddly enough, the Money-friendly Generation also holds anti-capitalist views in high esteem. Prior generations who witnessed the cold war and the fall of communism in eastern Europe regard capitalism as the victor in the war of ideologies. They believe that its advantages outweigh social problems stemming from capitalism. Millennials on the other hand have only experienced a capitalist society and take a much more critical view towards related issues. They are more sensitive to issues such as greed, inequity and polarization, and take note of companies that attempt to address such problems.

Money is vital in the modern age. However, when economic ideas go awry, they result in massive personal and social damages. Recently, investors were robbed and hoodwinked by promises of "guaranteed high returns," or were lured to try new forms of illegal gambling such as betting on the fluctuations of gold, silver and virtual currency prices. Experts emphasize the need to raise financial literacy and values through systemic education. Financial education is now incorporated into the curriculum of formal education around the world. What is encouraging is that the Money-friendly Generation has diligently learned about money and has emerged as consumers who are able to plan a balanced life for themselves. A new movement instigated by consumers to "hit companies with wads of cash," i.e., reward companies that are recognized for their good deeds by helping them raise their sales, is one such example of how a capitalist society can take self-correcting measures. Ultimately, it is up to the consumer to create an exemplary capitalist society. Such are the high expectations we place on the Money-friendly Generation in the age of V-nomics, and beyond.

COWBOY HERO

BEST WE PIVOT

"Pivoting" is often used in sports to refer to turning on an axis or central point, and in these post-COVID-19 times has come to mean a business transition. With changes in trends and an ever-evolving consumer market amid an escalating pandemic, a shrewd transition to an appropriate business model is a strategy that can make or break a company. Pivoting does not only mean a directional shift in times of crisis but has expanded to symbolize a major trend in business operations. It has come to represent a series of protocols, from setting hypotheses to conducting endless tests and course corrections, and is involved in all aspects of business operations, including manufacturing, strategy planning and marketing. Pivoting is imperative for startups armed with new items and technology, but it has also become unavoidable for larger, more established companies as they struggle in a volatile, uncertain, complex and ambiguous (VUCA) landscape.
Pivoting strategies can be divided into four groups depending on which resources are the focus of the business transition: (1) Core competency pivoting: changing a company's operations skills and know-how; (2) Hardware pivoting: centering on infrastructure, facilities and buildings; (3) Target pivoting: focusing on the existing clientele; and (4) Sales pivoting: consisting of designing new items and changing marketing channels.
A crisis is a capitalistic mechanism that helps weed out weaker enterprises. It's vital to note that companies that tear down existing markets and create new innovations are not those with innovative technology, but those that respond promptly to changes in consumer behavior. As we face a post-COVID-19 era of digital revolution, only companies that continually pivot can survive.
They need to pivot decisively in order to tackle an ever-changing market.

What do YouTube, Instagram, Twitter, and Netflix have in common?

"Online companies," "innovators that threaten the existing market," "platform companies," and numerous other descriptions come to mind. They share parallels in that they all began with initial business models that were not profitable, but then managed to effectively transition their businesses towards a path of success.

YouTube began as a dating site but failed to entice singles to share videos of themselves. It changed its strategy to accept all types of videos for public sharing, and the rest is history. Twitter was initially a podcast platform. However, when Apple offered podcast content for free, Twitter gained popularity by transforming itself into a message sharing service. Instagram had its roots as a cross between a gaming and a location-based social media service. They found gamers were more interested in sharing pictures, so they transitioned into a full social media business. Netflix began as a rental DVD delivery service and blossomed into the online movie streaming platform we all know.

These may sound like startup anecdotes, but it is difficult to find companies that have remained within their initial business parameters. As times and consumers changed, most companies overcame crisis after crisis by repeatedly changing the direction and purview of their business. "Pivoting" can be defined as efforts by corporations to transition their businesses to fully leverage its resources and aptly meet the unpredictable needs of customers.

The definition of "pivot" is "an axis or a central point on which something turns or balances." It is often used to describe a movement in sports such as basketball or volleyball when fixing one foot on the ground and turning the other in a different direction, preparing for the next move. Entrepreneur and business consultant Eric Ries, in his 2011 book *The Lean Startup*, first used the term "pivot" as part of business vernacular, defining it as "a structured course correction designed to test a new fundamental hypothesis about the product, strategy, and engine of growth." "Pivoting" henceforth was accepted as a formula for success. The term has emerged once again amid a global economic crisis triggered by COVID-19. The rampant spread of the virus shook consumer behavior to the core. Online purchases became part of our daily lives, and outdoor activities were brought inside the home. Lessons and meetings which were usually conducted face-to-face were done remotely. Restaurants, cafés, gyms and movie theaters lost customers every time governments announced stronger social distancing measures. Such changes became prevalent during the pandemic, but the shift was slowly taking place even before measures were put in place. The speed was so gradual that we were simply unaware of the transition.

Adapting to the new norm is critical not only for startups but also for all economic entities, from private businesses to industry giants. We have come to the realization that our very future will be under threat if we cannot change when faced with such a desperate crisis. We define "pivoting" as a series of protocols, from setting hypotheses to conducting endless tests and course corrections, which are involved in all aspects of business operations including manufacturing, strategy planning and marketing. Companies that boldly pivot, ready to take the leap beyond the current crisis and into a new age, can secure an opportunity for growth. Let's see how opportunities for business transitions in an age of revolution can be sought by examining and understanding the particulars and major subcategories of pivoting.

Characteristics of Pivoting

Pivoting is a form of innovation in which companies attempt to transition their business by various means to adapt to market changes. Innovation occurs when groundbreaking progress is made through new inroads into the economy.

<Pivoting versus Innovation>

		Consumers	
		Know what they want	Don't know what they want
Companies	Know what should be done (planned innovation)	Continuous innovation	Discontinuous innovation
	Don't know what should be done (experimental innovation)	Pivoting	Spin-off

Political economist Joseph Schumpeter's theory of evolutionary economics stipulates that innovation includes not only utilizing technological advances but also developing new markets and products, securing new resources, improving production processes, and introducing new systems. Pivoting becomes easier to understand when comparing it with existing definitions of innovation.

As shown in the table above, the market landscape can be divided into four categories based on "whether consumers are aware of or want the change," and "whether companies are mindful or certain of their countermeasures." Let's take a closer look at how pivoting differs from other concepts in this regard.

Focus on trials rather than planning

Companies, rather than consumers, usher in innovation. That's because even when consumer needs exist, innovation is not possible if a company hasn't developed the necessary technology. Therefore, companies progressively follow a technological roadmap to achieve innovation, and such a process is called "architectural innovation." This in turn can be divided into "Continuous innovation" and "Discontinuous innovation." Continuous innovation occurs when consumers know what they want. For instance, smartphones have increased their display size, extended their battery life, and become lighter in the course of their first, second and third generation iterations, exemplifying such incremental change. Discontinuous innovation, on the other hand, takes place when continuous innovations transcend to the next level, as demonstrated by the evolution from mobile phones to smartphones, and from film to digital cameras.

Pivoting differs from continuous and discontinuous innovation in that it centers not on planning but on trials. Rather than an innovation based on meticulous planning and execution, pivoting is a series of processes that involves an endless cycle of "hypothesis-execution(test)-correction-(re-)execution," and infinite course corrections to meet the sporadic needs of consumers. According to Professor Thales S. Teixeira, author of *Unlocking the Customer Value Chain: How Decoupling Drives Consumer Disruption*, the reason why companies fail is not because they lack innovation. Many companies believe they have been capsized in their rivals' wake of innovative technology, but in truth, the reason they flounder is because they were unable to respond to changes in consumer patterns. The main culprit of market destruction is not technological innovation but consumer choice. A company needs to overcome an unpredictable market plagued by VUCA (volatility, uncertainty, complexity and ambiguity) through continuous innovation based on an experimental spirit, i.e., pivoting.

Focus on a company-wide and immediate, rather than piecemeal, response

In experimental innovations, there are contrasts between pivoting and spin-offs, depending on the certitude of the consumer needs and the form of innovation. A "spin-off," which usually refers to a new storyline based on characters from an original movie or drama, is used in economic and business management terminology to indicate a separate start-up business of research personnel. Spin-offs become a coherent choice when neither the company nor the consumer can predict the viability of any innovation, allowing spin-offs to partially devise countermeasures.

If spin-offs sow the seeds of discovery for new opportunities, pivoting involves an immediate company-wide response. An attempt at a new strategy is immediately made and any errors are then corrected. "Strategy" is traditionally equated with "planning." However, according to Henry Mintzberg, an international authority on business management, planning is only one aspect of strategy. In fact, he advocates the need for an "emergent strategy": an improvised strategy based on the current situation.[1] By repeating successes and failures over time, a pattern will emerge and these patterns will collectively become the strategy. Then again, though responding immediately is important, it doesn't then mean that the emergent strategy can always be changed, willy-nilly.

In the words of Eric Ries, pivoting is "a change in strategy without a change in vision."[2] In an era of a speedy economy, where change is constant and nothing stands still, opportunities are fleeting and will pass by if one remains bogged down by the details. A swift response to the challenges faced can make or break a company.

Types of Pivoting

As previously outlined, the original definition of "pivot" lies in its axis. Pivoting, therefore, puts more emphasis on what is needed for the change (the axis), rather than on how much is to be changed (the amount of swiveling). Based on this axis for change, pivoting strategies can be divided into: (1) Core competency pivoting: changing a company's operations skills and operation know-how; (2) Hardware pivoting: centering on infrastructure, facilities and buildings; (3) Target pivoting: focusing on the existing clientele; and (4) Sales pivoting: consisting of designing new items and changing marketing channels. Let's take a closer look at each of these strategies in turn.

1. Core competency pivoting

Core competency pivoting involves shifting a company's business model to focus on its available capacity. As illustrated in the examples of YouTube, Instagram and Netflix, this is when startups flexibly change their business models according to market responses and is the most common form of pivoting in business. Baedal Minjok배달의 민족 is representative of core competency pivoting. Founder Kim Bong-jin's initial plan was to make a phone directory app. But setting up a database of phone numbers was an impossible task for him and his brother in the early stages of the company. He abandoned his initial plan for a nationwide directory service, targeting instead only the phone numbers for restaurants, which then naturally led to including orders and deliveries, giving shape to the current business model. The process allowed him to successfully pivot from "a mobile phone directory service" to "a mobile delivery service."

Noom 눔, a one-on-one coaching app that helps users correct their dietary and exercise habits, began as an offshoot of the CardioTrainer app launched in the U.S. in 2007, which utilized smartphones' GPS and accelerator sensors to calculate the user's workouts. Its developers discovered that among many app functions, the favorite feature was the "10,000 step counter," and thus devised a strategy to offer tips on improving users' diets and exercise, as well as continuous management plans for maintaining a healthy body. It successfully pivoted from a simple "measurement service" to a "care service" by going beyond analyzing users' exercise and dietary habits data to also providing coaching features that, with the support of relevant experts, monitor users' eating habits, exercise habits and overall health status.

Manufacturers can also adopt a pivoting strategy by applying their existing technology to venture into a new field. Zinus지누스 successfully applied its compression packaging technology, developed in its existing tent manufacturing business, to aid in shipping its mattresses. Mattresses are usually bulky and heavy and require specialists to deliver and install. Zinus caught on to the fact that single-person households found such deliveries troublesome, introducing the concept of "a mattress in a box," a first for the industry.[3] Once the compact package is opened, the mattress inflates to a normal size and therefore does not need a specialist for delivery and installation. The technology was also practical for international shipping and helped the brand become a bestseller on Amazon. Even with the pandemic wreaking havoc on sales of other manufacturers, its sales rose 18 percent year-on-year in the first quarter of 2020, while operational profits rose 4.1 percent.

Core competency pivoting can also transpire when a company applies its core expertise to diversify its business. As countries went into lockdown amid the spread of COVID-19, Grab, Southeast Asia's No.1 ride-hailing app, quickly mobilized its 149,000 drivers to offer food delivery services. Its drivers, who were facing inevitable unemployment, managed to continue working throughout the pandemic, and restaurants also managed to maintain sales through surging delivery orders. Grab's president Ming Maa predicted that "demand for delivery food will not go away once the coronavirus situation has stabilized," and disclosed plans to expand into delivery of daily necessities, concierge services using delivery agents, as well as transportation for medical emergencies. Its pivoting strategy focuses on transportation, branching out into finance and healthcare services.

2. Hardware pivoting

Hardware pivoting focuses on making use of material resources, such as a company's infrastructure, facilities and buildings, as a transition strategy. It suggests out-of-the-box ideas for new uses of its resources and offers new possibilities for their application, thereby providing a swift response to market demands. In August 2020, Taiwanese carriers Starlux Airlines and EVA Air began offering "flights to nowhere" in which passengers boarded a flight that took off, flew within Taiwanese controlled airspace, and then landed back at the same airport. Passengers get to "pretend to go abroad," enjoy air travel-related experiences like in-flight meals, entertainment and even duty-free shopping. Japan's ANA also offered 90-minute "cruise flights" that took off from and landed back at the same airport. These flight experiences will not likely make up for the gigantic losses that airlines suffered, but they may help ease the pain by bringing in some revenue through tickets and duty-free sales.

Korean Air and Asiana Airlines also converted their passenger jets into cargo carriers as demand for passenger flights plummeted, recording surprise profits in the second quarter of 2020, a successful example of hardware pivoting. Passenger carriers have had to seek diverse pivoting opportunities due to dwindling demand. Thai Airways opened an aircraft-themed restaurant within their headquarters in September 2020. The eatery installed actual seats from their business and economy-class sections. They also used Boeing 747 engines and windows as part of their tables, and installed an airstair at the entrance, making use of various aircraft parts in its interior design as well. Its pivoting offered a luxurious setting for customers who missed having in-flight meals.

Megabox

Museums take over the big screen at movie theaters. Cinemas are adopting such survival strategies through hardware pivoting.

Some companies have made new use of their manufacturing facilities as part of their pivoting strategy. As demand for beauty products slumped due to people wearing masks, cosmetics firms Kolmar Korea and COSMAX quickly transitioned part of their lines to manufacturing hand sanitizers in order to minimize losses.

Local cinema operators are also attempting to transition their businesses, making good use of their centrally located spaces. They began showing “alternative content,” such as operas, musicals, concerts, e-sports matches and lectures on their screens. Gone are the days when you only watched movies at your local cinema. In May 2020, CJ CGV screened the live concert of Metallica and the San Francisco Symphony, and concert fans, who were unable to enjoy international live acts due to COVID-19, flocked to the theater despite the fairly expensive 18,000 won ($15.50) tickets. Live broadcasts of e-sports matches, such as the ever-popular League of Legends, or finance management lectures for investment afficionados, are also featured on screening schedules. Megabox, through its "Cine Docent" project, also offered screenings of famous museum tours, featuring paintings and works of art from around the world for those who miss traveling abroad. Lotte Cinema screened performances of operas and ballets from the Royal Opera House of London in its "Opera in Cinema" program. The use of theaters to show something other than movies is not a new concept. Whereas previous attempts were one-off novelties, this transition will likely remain part of the cinema experience in the future.

The hospitality industry, including hotels, began seeking pivoting opportunities with its facilities and services. GLAD Hotels & Resorts and L'Escape Hotel were among the first to offer rooms as workspaces for those who could not go to their offices but were seeking to work away from their homes for various reasons, like having young children. These work-from-hotel guests would check in and out according to their regular office hours, rather than the usual 3 p.m. check-ins and 11 a.m. check-outs. The Conrad Seoul in Yeouido offered rooms with stationary bikes, yoga mats, weights, gym balls and pull-up bars for guests tired of working out at home, offering them a breathtaking view of the Han River while they enjoyed their training sessions. The Millennium Hilton Seoul offered a package that let parents de-stress from looking after their children all day. It joined hands with German educational toymaker Haba to turn their rooms into kids' play areas or "kids' cafés," filling them with toys and children's goods.

Hardware pivoting also allows for daring strategies such as transitioning to a completely new business. The Benikea Hotel in Jongno, downtown Seoul, converted its rooms into rental homes for young professionals in May 2019, a major transformation in its three-year history. The hotel abandoned its lodging business altogether and transformed its facilities as the number of Chinese visitors plummeted following bilateral disputes over the deployment of the THAAD missile defense system. In the U.K., LOWE Guardians, a property management company, launched its "SHED project" in 2017, pivoting vacant buildings by installing self-contained homes within them. These micro homes can be assembled like IKEA furniture, using a hammer and drill, and then placed in empty properties such as warehouses and office blocks.[4] This garnered public attention as a creative solution to the problem of abandoned buildings, while providing affordable housing to those who are seeking to live within the city. Hardware pivoting, which makes use of a company's physical resources, will no longer be seen as a novel attempt or temporary strategy, but will likely become a vital strategy for a company's, and an industry's, survival.

3. Target pivoting

Target pivoting seeks a business transition as a swift response to ever-changing needs, based on a list of and information about its existing clientele. Customers are an important asset that forms the backbone of a company. However, when unforeseen calamities such as COVID-19 occur, customer needs will inevitably change. If companies do not respond quickly to such change, customers will not just make a one-off purchase but will likely be completely driven away from a particular commercial domain, making it nearly impossible for companies to make up their losses. Therefore, it behooves companies to briskly transition their businesses to avail themselves of the knowledge they have gleaned about their target base, which they undoubtedly have carefully studied, to minimize the possibility of losing their customers altogether.

ES Golf Tour operates premium overseas golf packages and acts as a booking agent for flights, lodging and country club access. As with many agencies, it was hit hard by the coronavirus outbreak, and had to halt all of its tours leading to most of its staff going on unpaid leave. They considered switching their focus to local golf packages, but that market was already saturated, rife with cutthroat competition, and profit margins were basically impossible with just local bookings. When faced with an urgent need to devise a new business direction, ES Golf Tour finally realized that its most valuable asset was its list of VIP clients. This was not just a collection of names but an overall knowledge database, gleaned from numerous overseas packages, about how to meet the needs of premium customers. The company realized that its premium clients wanted not just booking agents but a complete "door-to-door service" from their home to the country club and back. They immediately formed network partnerships with chauffeur service providers, as well as car rental shops, and introduced a new concept of premium golf packages that included previously unheard-of services in the domestic market, such as temporary and one-way chauffeurs, thus successfully pivoting their operations.

MyRealTrip, a free travel platform, also shifted its focus from overseas to domestic tour packages at the start of the outbreak. They had anticipated that travel buffs would quickly turn their focus to local destinations. MyRealTrip organized their travel destinations into categories such as gourmet, spa and golf packages, and invested in technology that helped their customers pick out a destination depending on their personal preferences. Such efforts helped daily average reservations rebound to 3,000 in August 2020 from below 40 earlier in the year at the start of the pandemic. It racked up sales of 5 billion won ($4.3 million) in July alone, successfully pivoting its business by adapting to the change in customer needs.[5]

Some companies have even completely changed their business content while targeting existing clientele. When faced with dwindling sales, Creatrip크리에이트립, a platform that provides travel information about Korea to tourists, launched a proxy shopping service한국 직구 for overseas customers. Foreign guests who had bought clothing, cosmetics, food products, kitchenware and other items in their previous visits to Korea were able to purchase the same products through the platform's web site. In April, Creatrip partnered with influencers on social media to produce a proxy shopping channel, which racked up an accumulative 120,000 views. It plans to expand its foreign language services to include English, Japanese and Thai.[6]

4. Sales pivoting

The final category is sales pivoting, which consists of designing new items and changing marketing channels. The transition from offline to online sales routes, including the omni-channel strategy, was already an emerging trend in the market. Sales pivoting includes such shifts by retailers that transform their business by focusing more on online channels, as well as efforts by companies previously not focused on product design and sales who pivot their businesses in response to radical changes in the market.

Lotte Hotel

A hotel's pivoting strategy, in a bid to make up for plunging revenue due to a steep drop in tourists. Lotte Hotel's He:on Premium Shop, selling its own merchandise including beddings and towels.

Airline companies, previously more focused on passenger and carrier flights, are opting to diversify their businesses by offering what used to be their supplementary service as their main source of revenue. Canada's Air North launched a service to deliver microwavable frozen airplane food to customers in the country's northwesternmost province, Yukon. Its primary clients are those who miss inflight meals, and also those who want to stock up on ready-to-eat meals during a prolonged lockdown. Australia's Qantas Airways released its "Qantas Care Pack" for sale from its online Rewards Store, putting together a first-class package that includes sleepwear, an amenity kit, as well as snacks and teabags. Such an enterprise may have begun as an attempt to prevail over the pandemic, but if they persevere in their efforts, it may just be the steppingstone to diversify their operations, such as the manufacture and sales of their own private brand products.

The hotel industry has also been trying to bounce back from losses by pushing supplementary services to the fore. In May 2020, Lotte Hotel Seoul opened its "He:on해온 Premium Shop" on the first floor, stocking it with its own products including hotel bedding sets, towels and bath gowns that are usually provided in the hotel rooms. Most Korean hotels offer their products for sale, but this was the first time that a hotel actually opened a store to sell their products.

Local suppliers of food and agricultural goods for school kitchens had to desperately find other sales avenues as schools effectively closed down in 2020. Farms that supply organic and eco-friendly agricultural goods to school kitchens usually keep to strict schedules for cultivating and harvesting their produce, as stipulated in contracts, because the products are more expensive to procure than conventionally grown produce. As students were forced to stay at home and attend lessons remotely, these suppliers faced a bleak future of having to discard most of their produce or sell them for a fraction of the price. The Gyeonggi AgroFood Institute launched sales of single-portion meal kits made with organic produce, helping these suppliers pivot from a business-to-business (B2B) model to a business-to-consumer

(B2C) model. The institute is also planning to launch a "farm product package" subscription service that will send packages to customers in the form of gifts.

Background : The Advent of the "Economy of Speed"

Many of the different types of pivoting came to be as companies strove desperately to seek avenues to survive in the aftermath of COVID-19. Pivoting became a key strategy for industries hit hardest by the pandemic, such as travel and tourism, arts and culture. However, the key point is that many of these companies were concerned about their futures even before the outbreak, faced with major upheavals in the current age, such as the digital transformation. According to an Accenture survey, 93 percent of global executives felt that their viability was under threat because their companies could not keep pace with the speed of change in the market.[7] COVID-19 only accelerated a chain of events that was leading to changes in consumer lifestyles and buying patterns, prompting business transitions that resulted in innovations in sales channels.

Our society has already evolved into "an economy of speed" from "an economy of scale." In an economy of scale, where selling as many well-made products as possible maximizes profit, it is important to manufacture the optimal product through meticulous planning in order to minimize the possibility of failure. On the other hand, in an economy of speed, where consumer needs change constantly, testing hypotheses becomes key as companies must respond swiftly in an uncertain world by first providing products and services and then quickly making corrections to their plans based on customer feedback. This is because consumer needs are continually changing, even during the course of this drawn-out process.

Creating an environment that supports pivoting

We should note that the current environment encourages businesses to pivot through brisk transitions. Previously, companies often encountered restrictions and missed out on opportunities for major innovation. Progress was inevitably slow as they were in charge of the whole process, including meticulous planning and execution. But times have since changed. With external assistance, pivoting is now feasible even if companies are not completely ready. Cloud computing is one such example: a company no longer has to set up an entire server and manage data since it receives the necessary infrastructure from the cloud service provider while correcting and improving upon its required services.

Companies can now also outsource core business operations, such as planning, support and operations, going beyond the commonly outsourced operations or subcontract production through original equipment manufacturers (OEMs). For instance, such outsourced tasks can range from collaborating with university labs on research and development through open innovation, to recruiting communications firms for marketing and PR, to also hiring sales agents to sell products to consumers face-to-face. The current business landscape has allowed for all these factors to move in unison once a company settles on the direction to which it wishes to pivot.

Outlook and Implications

— Bracing for the make-or-break "Kodak moment"

A crisis is a capitalistic mechanism that helps weed out weaker enterprises. The top 25 percent of U.S. businesses saw their stock prices gain 6 percent weathering three economic recessions, whereas that of the bottom 25 percent tumbled 44 percent.[8] Short-sighted companies will fall sharply behind the more discerning ones. Korean companies are also following in the same vein, as 11 out of the top 15 conglomerate flagships saw their sales decline in the first half of 2020.[9] Finally, we will take a look at how companies should prepare for a successful pivot to overcome the current crisis and use it as a foothold for a new leap forward.

The ability to test hypotheses and to learn from failures

Firstly, businesses must constantly set hypotheses and test them to seek pivoting opportunities. In truth, the success of a pivot is difficult to predict. This is why it becomes so important to constantly examine the direction of possible pivots, making use of diverse methods.

A/B testing, often used in the decision-making stage, can provide a direction for pivoting. Netflix, for example, used two different designs for its homepage in an A/B test to determine which would draw a larger audience, and thus succeeded in boosting viewer ratings by 20 to 30 percent.

Secondly, the organization must adopt a flexible culture that allows for failures that will ultimately lead to a successful pivot. According to Richard Foster, a senior lecturer at Yale University and former director at innovation consulting firm Innosight, the speed of innovation at larger enterprises is slower than changes taking place in the market.[10] Startups need to change their direction within a limited budget and immediately consider the feedback it receives in their course corrections, allowing for a more versatile strategy. Most big corporations, on the other hand, set up future plans on an annual basis. Planning and execution are far removed from one another in their expansive organizations, the structures of which are often bureaucratic. A company's return on investment (ROI), commonly used as a performance indicator, is also a key factor for a company's hesitation in making transitions. A daring pivot, born from a repetitive cycle of "corrective implementation and re-execution," needs an injection of a return of failure (ROF) perspective, in which a company can learn from its mistakes. In an age of tumultuous change, it is no longer important whether you fail, but what you have learned from that failure.

Thirdly, various regulations need to be realigned to allow for rapid pivoting. Even when companies need to push through a vital pivot to overcome a crisis, they are often faced with regulations that bog down the process. For example, some agencies that specialized in overseas travel began to attract customers by arranging domestic package tours without proper registration. It was nearly impossible to embark on the complex procedure of amending existing regulations and articles of the Tourism Promotion Act, nor was it considered fair to existing domestic tour operators. Nobel Prize-winning economist Milton Friedman said it was difficult for a government to find an optimal time to intervene in the market, likening it to a "fool in the shower." When the fool turns the hot water on, it takes a while to heat up, so the fool simply turns up the hot water all the way, scalding himself, and then quickly turning on the cold water.[11] If the government takes the side of one party, setbacks are inevitable. Governments will have to wrestle with introducing prompt regulatory changes that enable companies to pivot and prevail over threats to their survival.

Speedy Rejection and Adaptation

Finally, the most important factors for a successful pivot are making bold decisions and having the courage to persuade the relevant people. Pivoting includes the sunk cost of abandoning the time and money poured into the process. This involves accepting failures and persuading company staff, investors and existing customers. Slack, a widely popular business communication platform, has its roots in an online game called "Glitch." Its developer launched the massively multiplayer online role-playing game (MMORPG) in 2011, but failed to grab gamers' attention, ending up halting the service the following year. Because the company's staff were scattered in different locations, in Vancouver, San Francisco and New York, they needed a business messaging tool to communicate with one another. Stewart Butterfield, head of the company, realized the tool's potential and completely transitioned its business from gaming to a communication platform, after officially apologizing to his investors, customers and other involved parties. Butterfield confessed that his game had failed to lure in users and voiced his sincere concern for the livelihoods of the company's staff, and also shared information that may be helpful for the existing game members after the service ended. Such sincerity allowed his company to successfully pivot without suffering from any backlash.

When Kodak was synonymous with cameras and photographs, a "Kodak moment" used to represent a brilliant split-second photo opportunity to capture a model or object. For most of the 20th century, Kodak remained smug in its position as a leader in the world of ever-profitable film and ignored the advances made in digital camera technology. Its complacent attitude toward changing market needs ultimately resulted in its bankruptcy. A "Kodak moment" has now become the equivalent of a make-or-break moment for a company that has (or hasn't) the foresight in an age of tumultuous change.[12] The year 2021 is presenting many companies with their own "Kodak moment," following the COVID-19 outbreak and the digital revolution. The market never stands still and is constantly on the move, evolving like a living creature. Companies need to boldly pivot and meet the ever-changing market head on.

COWBOY HERO

ON THIS ROLLER COASTER RIDE

Generation Z, those born after 1995 and ranging from their mid-teens to mid-twenties, enjoy an entirely different lifestyle from their older counterparts. They take on random "challenges" on social media with gusto, respond to the unusual, relish the unconventional, and yet are quick to lose interest and move on to their next fixation. Fads flare up then fizzle out just as quickly. Such tendencies are comparable to riding a roller coaster. Gen Zers latch on to the latest craze and enjoy them with others, then jump on to the next thrill, as if switching rides at an amusement park.

We call this the "Roller Coaster Life," or the "RC Life," and those who revel in the lifestyle, "RC Riders." These young consumers are inevitably drawn to and take part in trendy events and challenges as if lining up at a queue outside an attraction. They hanker after fleeting diversions and novel collaborations that go beyond the scope of reasonable expectation, as if delighting in the unpredictable speed of roller coasters, only to quickly pivot to the next frenzy once the previous fad loses its luster.

The advent of the RC Ride lifestyle coincides with Gen Z's thirst for getting involved, seeking out thrills in their everyday lives. As digital natives with itchy feet, they roam in search of newer, more thrilling content, while clutching their smartphones. The RC Ride is no longer a youthful whim but an indication of a market change that companies need to embrace. It has become all the more imperative for them to adopt a fast lifecycle strategy to anticipate customers' trends in guerilla-style, hit-and-run short-term marketing, rather than agonizing over a foolproof, long-term marketing strategy.

#1 University student A is in the middle of practicing a routine for an upcoming dance challenge. After about half an hour of practice, the student sets up a smartphone on a tripod and records the routine. It's also fun to observe the feedback after uploading the video on social media. It even brings a sense of satisfaction for being part of the "in" crowd.

***#2**. High school student B enjoys eating jelly candy. Pork belly-shaped jelly candy, and pickled radish-shaped jelly candy are some of the more unusual and bizarre releases that stood out in a recent visit to a nearby convenience store. Rather than the usual flavors, these were the picks of the day. It's not important whether they are tasty. That they provide amusement is in itself quite gratifying.*

This is how Gen Zers amuse themselves. They flock to complete random challenges, respond to the unique and enjoy the unconventional. When the fad fizzles soon after, they move on to the next trend. The older generations grumble that they find it difficult to understand young people these days. There may not be a formal name for this group, but those ranging from their mid-teens to mid-twenties, usually born after 1995, are collectively called "Generation Z," "Gen Z" or "Gen Zers." They follow Gen X, born during the 1970s, and Gen Y, better known as "millennials," born during the 1980s and early 1990s. Whatever they are called, the newest batch of young people are certainly different. Why is that?

Let's imagine that you're riding a roller coaster. You wait in line with pounding anticipation and, when it's your turn, join the crowd to get on board. The safety bars lower, the ride slowly moves forward, and then screams and shrieks fill the air as you're tossed, flipped and turned during the ride. Before you know it, it's over, and the attendees welcome you back and gesture toward the exit. The ride was short but sweet, so you disembark with little regret. You take the exit and go in search of the next ride in the amusement park.

The lifestyle of Gen Z is akin to riding a roller coaster. They flit around fleeting trends, take part in them with others, then soon after set off for the next diversion in the same manner as riding amusement park rides. We call this kind of lifestyle of Gen Z the "Roller Coaster Life," or the "RC Life," and those who revel in the lifestyle, "RC Riders."

RC Riders find it amusing to take part in the latest challenges and feel a sense of belonging when they flock together as a group to see the latest product. They briefly rave about unique collaborations rather than conventional products, and always seek out new trends by chasing after diverse products rather than staying loyal to one single brand. They cannot abide by the boredom of an unvarying routine, and their search cycle for new thrills gets shorter and shorter. The trend can no longer be brushed aside as a youthful whim but rather heralds a general change in the market that we need to note and counter. Let's take a look at the RC Ride lifestyle that has pervaded all areas of our society and how it has affected the industry.

The RC Ride: Enjoying Life like Riding a Roller Coaster

"A tragedy in landscape. A comedy in portrait."

This was attached as a comment to Rain's '*Gang*깡' music video on YouTube. The video may not seem much when viewed in landscape mode on a smartphone, but when flipped to portrait mode and watched with comments, it becomes hilarious. The music video may have been a flop when it was released three years ago, but by 2020 the song returned to the charts as the comment section became a new playground for viewers. The driving force behind the song's popularity is not its music video but its comments section. Rarely does anyone watch the music in full screen; most people click on the music video to watch it along with the comments. This gave rise to the term "One '*Gang*' a Day," prompting viewers to watch the music video at least once a day.

When the comment section becomes more entertaining than the main content, it becomes a "hot spot for comments 댓글맛집." The early days of such recreations took place on the "DC Inside" website, where young people uploaded pictures, commented on them and replied to one another. "Title Institute제목학원" on Facebook is another site in which people gave amusing titles to interesting and unique pictures and photos. YouTube's comments section is an upgrade of the two forms of entertainment. If the former were mere replies to the content provided, today's comments section on YouTube allows the audience to "excavate" fringe content and push it into the mainstream. The audience will ingest the content as much as they want and then, once weary, move on to the next thing.

With such a phenomenon, we see the advent of the "meme." A "meme" was a term coined by British evolutionary biologist Richard Dawkins in his 1976 book *The Selfish Gene* to exemplify the self-replicating concept of cultural elements, much like a gene. The term is now more commonly used to describe images or visual content that has been given new meaning, and, as such, has far-reaching impact in online communities and on social media.

The crux of a meme lies in willing participation, intense fun, and a short lifespan. Meme creators voluntarily reproduce content and derive satisfaction from the process. Dead content comes back to life in their hands and is born anew and spread in this "perfect consumer-centered new market."

There are three stages to the RC Life. The first is "The Queue." Waiting to take part in the latest fad is similar to people waiting in line for a roller coaster ride. The second stage is "The Ride." The erratic up-and-down and round-and-round movements of the journey are electrifying and exhilarating. The ride is similar to that of Gen Z consumer patterns in that they seek new and unpredictable diversions. The last stage is "The Departure." Once the ride is over, you may feel a tinge of regret, but only briefly; then you disembark and move on to the next ride. The cycle for today's trends is brief, and once over, another takes hold. Let's take a more in-depth look at these three stages of the RC Life and how they have pervaded every aspect of our lives.

1. The Queue: Many people are lining up - so must I

After the first measure, you shyly raise each index finger in the air, one at a time. Then you wave and pump both arms to the beat in a lively dance, dancing on your own or in a group. Such was the "Any Song Challenge" spawned by the release of Zico's 'Any Song', which topped the digital sales, downloads and streaming charts in Korea in the first half of 2020. Its popularity was driven by the "Any Song Challenge" which spread like wildfire on social media. More than 100,000 uploads of 50-second videos flooded TikTok, garnering a combined 106 million views.[1] There have been many cases of viral marketing upon single and album releases in the past. But what made the "Any Song Challenge" so different? It was a dance that virtually anyone could follow. The repetitive flailing of the arms, minus any lower-body movement, allowed even those who can't dance well to take part in the fun, granting a sense of virtual community. In amusement parks, people are more attracted to rides with long lines. When you see such a line, you immediately think, "Ooh, this should be fun," and join the queue, resulting in a line that grows even longer.

Such challenges were not limited to dance. The spread of COVID-19 prompted the #stayathomechallenge which allowed many to enjoy the little pleasures in life. The "Dalgona Coffee Challenge" was one such example, spurring the young and old to spend considerable time and energy whipping – hundreds or even a thousand times – a mixture of instant coffee, sugar and hot water into a meringue-like consistency. They would then take "proofies" of their endeavor and upload them on social media with hashtags such as #homecafe or #stayathomechallenge as a form of playful diversion.

Companies have taken note of customers' need to participate in creating their fun and have applied it to their marketing strategies. The food and beverage industry in particular has embraced this trend. Dong-A Otsuka동아오츠카 recently accepted applications for its sixth round of fan club members for their Oronamin-C energy drink through a challenge. Applicants were asked to take photos or videos to express their personality using the energy drink as a prop, then upload them on social media. Naturally, RC Riders took up the challenge and turned in more than 18,000 submissions.[2] Global lemon- and lime-flavored soft drink brand Sprite teamed up with local social media influencers with 1 million followers or more and launched the #Be_Yourself dance challenge#거침없이챌린지 for its Korean audience, raking in 27 million views.[3] These various "challenges" have become an arena for stress-free entertainment for the younger generation to break the weary and lethargic monotony of social distancing.

Memes are becoming more prevalent in advertisements as well. Burger King Korea, a frontrunner in meme campaigns, parodied a scene from the 2003 hit drama *Age of Wanderers*야인시대, in which the protagonist repeats the phrase "four dollars" in a stubborn negotiation tactic. The popular ad racked up 6 million views on YouTube. The burger chain then parodied a line from the Korean movie *Tazza*타짜 in which a gambler shouts, "Double or nothing!" The view count for the ad hit 7 million. It doesn't end there. The aforementioned "One '*Gang*' a Day" meme became such a phenomenon that snack giant Nongshim농심 signed on the artist Rain to star in their latest ad campaign for their "*ggang*깡", or "crunch," series of snacks, including shrimp, potato and sweet potato flavors, the names of which all end in "*-ggang*." Sales of the snacks for July exceeded an all-time high of 10 billion won ($8.5 million).[4]

Social distancing may have been drawn out, but apps that reflected the needs of RC Riders have evolved. Lovely Market러블리마켓 emerged as the go-to shopping app for young women in 2020. Tens of thousands of women flock to its sporadic offline flea markets, where they shop and socialize.[5] Lovely Market users call themselves "LM Buffs러덕" and socialize in chat rooms to share the latest fashion news. Such a sense of kinship and belonging leads to brand loyalty for Lovely Market in which users are all too eager to open their wallets. The key to Lovely Market's success is communication and interaction.

As with the increase in RC Riders who value communication and interaction, there has been an increase in "live commerce," in which sellers communicate with buyers in real time. Customers send in comments for the models to, for example, "wear the yellow dress" or "show the back," and can experience the appeal of obtaining real-time information on a featured product.

The buzz over live commerce has prompted offline retailers such as department and convenience stores to jump on the bandwagon. Hyundai Department Store's one-hour live commerce session of "G-Cut" apparel brought in the equivalent of 30 percent of the fashion brand's monthly sales. CU, the convenience store chain, sold out 30,000 ice-cream cups in two hours of a live commerce stream.[6] IT giants Naver and Kakao made their forays into the platform in 2020, respectively launching "Naver Selective" and "Kakao Shopping Live." It will be interesting to see what the future holds for the live commerce industry.

2. The Ride: Reveling in the unpredictable speed

Once the roller coaster ride begins, the fun lies in its unpredictable speed. The track twists and turns and the rider, unprepared for what's to come, is awarded with short yet electrifying thrills. RC Riders feel weary of recurring or predictable patterns and continually yearn for fresh changes in their routines. As such, brief and unexpected deviations, or "spin-offs" grab the attention of RC Riders.

Such is the driving force behind the popularity of short YouTube variety shows, as opposed to the longer equivalents on television. For example, three protagonists of MBC Network's reality TV program *I Live Alone*나혼자 산다, Park Na-rae, Han Hye-jin and Hwasa, have created alter egos Georgina, Samantha and Maria to star in their more scintillating online spinoff called *Women's Secret Party*여은파.

Flour meets fashion. Young consumers rave over such unconventional collaborations.

Daehan Flour Mills, Musinsa

Such diversions are not limited to media content. RC Riders' pursuit of new stimulation led to the 2020 craze for unconventional collaborations. RC Riders don't respond to things that are merely pretty and chic. They enthuse about one-off collaborations between hitherto unrelated items that dare to break the mold. Daehan Flour Mills, the maker of the Gompyo곰표 (곰=bear) line of flour products, was successful in creating buzz through its collaboration with clothing retailer 4XR when they released padded winter jackets emblazoned with the retro green logo, taking social media by storm. This led to similar runs of Gompyo T-shirts as well as cushions. Daehan also teamed up with 7bräu to release Gompyo Wheat Beer for sale through CU convenience stores, which sold 100,000 cans in just three days.[7] The pairing may seem unconventional, yet it satisfied the needs of RC Riders who revel in the unfamiliar and entertaining.

Gompyo's success has paved the way for "food fashion," and collaborations between food and fashion brands. Sandwich chain Subway released a line of apparel with their menu and recipes stamped onto a background of green, yellow and white. Beer and soju giant HiteJinro teamed up with the young fashion brand Covernat to release a popular line of casualwear and accessories sporting its famous blue toad logo. Such unexpected collaborations and releases have achieved increasing popularity.

3. The Departure: And when it's over, no regrets

An article on an online community bulletin board was making the rounds: "A death notice for the '*Gang*' game." When the "One '*Gang*' a Day" phenomenon was featured on the eight o'clock news, the author whined that it was its official death knell. Ironically, a meme fizzles out when it achieves mainstream status. If everyone becomes aware of a meme, it quickly loses its subtle and unique allure. A distinct characteristic of a meme is its limited shelf life. The general public move on to the next one once its infatuation with a meme runs its course.

In the past, when a drama series posted high ratings, broadcasters used to schedule in additional episodes or specials to maintain audience interest. The viewers themselves also requested more episodes of their favorite show. However, these days additional episodes no longer attest to the popularity of a series. Viewers were taken aback by news that the popular TV series *When the Camellia Blooms* would add another eight episodes, and immediately flooded the broadcaster, KBS, with concerned messages and e-mails. It ultimately turned out to be fake news, but it still illustrates changes in viewing trends. No matter how popular a series may be, it needs a satisfactory conclusion to allow its audience to bid a sweet farewell.

Other storytellers have opted for the multi-seasonal format, in which a series would go on hiatus and return with a second season, rather than prolonging the series with additional episodes, allowing for the unpacking of a new story. The seasonal drama was a system that used to be largely regarded as foreign and impossible to implement in Korea. Now it has become an accepted format, with 2020 seeing the launch of the first seasons of tvN's *Hospital Playlist* and *Stranger*, as well as the second season of Netflix's Korean-language drama *Kingdom*. Seasonal dramas meet the needs of RC Riders in that, even with the end of the first season, one can seek the stimuli of another drama with no time to be bored, all the while looking forward to the second season.

The online gaming industry has also adopted the seasonal format in which, after a certain period, the developer resets data and adds new content for a fresher gaming experience. In fact, it is difficult for a game to provide continuous enjoyment for an unlimited period. Developers seek to prolong the life of a game and hold on to existing gamers' attention, as well as to grab new customers through this system. League of Legends is a prime example, with each January marking the start of a new season that ends in November. Gamers' ranks are reset, but rewards are distributed in January according to the ranks of the previous season. Diablo III and Path of Exile have also adopted the seasonal format, allowing users to enjoy a renewed experience.

Such "ending aesthetics" are all the more prominent among limited-edition items. A successful marketing for limited editions leads to a product being completely sold out. The summer of 2020 saw long lines in front of Starbucks stores in Korea, even before opening hours, amid a frenzy for their "summer-ready bags." Hollys Coffee's offer of a multipurpose folding cart, and Dunkin's Nordisk Folding Box, emerged as "it" items and opened an era of limited-edition goods. Their limited nature raises their value, and fierce competition for the products ensues. Once obtained, the products are displayed as spoils of war in "proofies" on social media. Due to their rarity and novelty, combined with the desire to show them off, the popularity of limited editions is unlikely to wane. "Resales" of such products (see Chapter 7) have also recently picked up, adding even more value to products whose limited runs have an end in sight.

Why They Ride the Roller Coaster

The advent of the RC Ride lifestyle can be delineated along generational and environmental factors.

First off, Gen Zers undeniably have a high level of "self-efficacy," a concept proposed by Canadian-American psychologist Albert Bandura to define a belief or expectation of a person's ability to execute courses of action. The consumer's active participation stems from the firm belief that it will result in a payoff, be it in the form of enjoyment, learning or a sense of community. Gen Zers readily take part in online activities with the expectation of making friends. Their perceptions of camaraderie differ from those of older generations. Camaraderie is no longer simply limited to friends and colleagues who share the same space within a school or a workplace. It now includes online acquaintances and relationships based on empathy and solidarity over common hobbies or inclinations.

Secondly, Gen Z grew up well provided for compared to the older generations, and thus have higher expectations for their quality of life. However, they also suffer from anxiety stemming from a recession and a high unemployment rate. With COVID-19 woes encroaching on their everyday lives, they seek exhilarating thrills in their spending routines as a means to escape from their stagnant reality. As an inherent rebellion against the stern, solemn and serious nature of the older generations, they place more value on the fun and the frivolous. They seek to recharge by leading an RC Ride lifestyle that puts emphasis entirely on amusement.

And finally, Gen Z is the first generation to be born into a world of digital and technological advances, evolving from "digital natives" to "digital bohemians." Mobile technology was already a part of their lives from the moment of their birth and has since been a central part of their lives. They make use of smart technology in communications, shopping, leisure and all aspects of their routines, and are more accustomed to watching YouTube than television, jumping from content to content in short intervals. The explosion of TikTok on social media is in line with such trends. As such, Gen Zers are familiar with navigating through the latest fads, maneuvering with speed and flexibility, with an uncomplicated mindset and yet a short attention span. As digital natives with itchy feet, they never settle down, but rather continually roam here and there in search of shorter, more thrilling experiences. These "digital bohemians" are familiar with paying minimal attention to one item before quickly moving on to the next; this applies not only to their viewing habits, but also to their buying habits.

The nature of Gen Z is interlaced with an environment that breeds an ever-shorter RC Ride cycle. In the current age of abundance – the highest in human history – consumers are more driven by enjoyment rather than by need. This is the reason behind the paradigm of "the economy of obsolescence" that has taken hold amid an endless oversupply of new products. French economist and philosopher Serge Latouche points out in his 2011 book, *Vers une société d'abondance frugal* Towards a Frugal Abundant Society, that companies often compel consumers to spend more through built-in obsolescence to create more demand. Planned or built-in obsolescence is a policy of designing a product with an artificially limited lifespan to enable future releases of new models that differ little from existing ones.

As differentiating one product from the next becomes more difficult, psychological obsolescence comes to the fore through fashion and advertising to induce consumers to replace their existing possessions. In other words, companies inundating the market with advertisements and the constant updates in fashion trends in the media induce a shorter replacement cycle for consumer goods.

Short-form content and advances in communication technology have also played a crucial role in the development of the trend. TikTok hailed the advent of numerous short-form platforms which entice the consumer to continually enjoy new content through video recommendations that utilize AI-based technology. Developers are finding ways to provide consumers with novel content through advances in AR or VR technologies. That is to say, Gen Z's tendency to seek out better thrills by navigating from content to content has become even stronger amid an oversupply of goods and information. Such generational and environmental properties have elevated the RC Ride from a minor issue to a major trend.

Outlook and Implications

— The Importance of a Company's Fast Lifecyle Strategy

If anyone brushed aside the RC Ride as merely a youthful whim in the past, it is time for that thinking to change. Youth trends will more than likely be disseminated to successive generations and will ultimately become the accepted norm. Companies will need to formulate a strategy to counter an ever-increasing number of RC Riders who seek out more intense thrills in shorter cycles.

Life history theory, based on biological evolution, seeks to explain how various aspects of anatomy and behavior have been shaped through natural selection. It can be divided into "fast" and "slow" lifecycle strategies. The theory dictates that an individual who grows up in a predictable environment will likely choose the slow lifecycle strategy, which puts higher emphasis on future gains. On the other hand, those who grew up in an unpredictable setting will likely opt for the fast lifecycle strategy, which accentuates immediate gains.[8] For example, when long-term prospects remain murky at best amid the spread of COVID-19, more people will tend to choose a "fast lifecycle strategy," replacing a future-goal oriented lifestyle with one that places more emphasis on the present.

Let's apply this to business practices. A product or business model needs to go through an arduous process that begins with identifying the customer's needs, targeting a niche, developing ideas, securing alternatives, concept planning, consumer research, predictions on product demand, selecting a key function, choosing the design and securing a distribution network. Products that follow such a protocol are improved upon or give way to subsequent models depending on market feedback. The overall procedure can be called a lifecycle or a life-history cycle of a product. In stable market conditions, companies required meticulous and long-term planning because they were under pressure to develop a failproof product and provide a satisfactory return on investment (ROI); therefore, a slow lifecycle strategy was inevitable. However, as fashion cycles grow shorter, the slow lifecycle strategy is not enough for companies to match the pace of the latest trends. The market and its consumers will already have moved on by the time a product is released. So, a fast lifecycle strategy is crucial for a company to provide its customers with fresher stimulation while taking an acceptable level of risk in the midst of rapidly changing surroundings.

The fast lifecycle strategy isn't only relevant to small startups. In fact, it is vital to veteran companies as well.

What's an "RtA"? Consumers enjoy sources of fleeting amusement.

Nongshim, the nation's leading maker of instant noodles, may have a solid line of long-term steady sellers such as Shin Ramyun, Neoguri and Chapaghetti, but it never ceases to release new brands with fun flavors to entice their customers. One such example was "Angry RtA." "RtA" was once a nickname for Neoguri너구리 because when non-Koreans read the Korean label upside-down, the letters seem to read "RtA." The ramyun maker amped up the spice level for the limited edition by three times that of the original Neoguri and succeeded in selling more than 4 million packages within two weeks of its release, skyrocketing to the No. 3 position on the company's bestseller list.[9] Such "hit-and-run" releases instill a youthful and dedicated corporate image, especially among its younger clientele.

Short-term Marketing: I don't know what you'll like, so here's a bit of everything

RC Ride trends require an endless series of guerilla-style, hit-and-run short-term marketing gimmicks, however flawed they may be, rather than a meticulously planned long-term marketing strategy. Some products that make use of short-term marketing rarely last more than three months because the market is inundated with new releases and promotions that lead to shorter trend cycles. A market led by RC Riders no longer fosters the concept of a "mega-hit" brand. There are products that enjoy popularity and are sold out for a limited period. The product requires a subsequent strategy to hold on to consumer interest, or it will soon fall behind. Quantity trumps all in short-term marketing, focusing on rapid and frequent bursts of promotions.

Convenience stores are masters of short-term marketing. CU attempted a singular marketing strategy in 2020, centered around the myth of Dangun, the founder of the first Korean kingdom, Gojoseon. It took inspiration from the bear, the tiger, garlic and mugwort that feature in the national foundation story, and released a "Tiger Latte," "Gomyo (as in "bear") Popcorn", mugwort rice cake popsicles, and packets of minced garlic as part of its short-term marketing package. What was eye-catching was the phrase that described the new products: "Dangun products in a stream of consciousness." In other words, the chain was admitting that there was little rhyme or reason to the marketing scheme for these four products. In fact, the laid-back promotion only lasted two weeks. Although it seemed unpolished and haphazard, the response was unexpectedly positive. Sales of the four products jumped, including that of the minced garlic which rose 45 percent, even though it was not usually among the convenience store's steady sellers.[10] It was a gimmick tailor-made for RC Riders and Gen Zers, who prefer to make fun and novel purchases.

Musinsa, an online clothing platform popular among those in their 20s, uploaded more than 66,000 new items in 2019 alone.[11] It also launched its Musinsa TV channel on YouTube, providing styling tips, brand stories, and a variety of near endless content. It's as though the company were telling its customers, "I wasn't sure what you wanted, so here's a bit of everything." The company is serving up pretty much everything on a platter and it's up to buyers to pick and choose what they want. Others that follow the trend include online retailers such as 29CM, Zigzag and W Concept, which provide an endless stream of content at intermittent intervals. Gone are the days when companies painstakingly curated a single event to foster a mega-hit product. The marketing of today focuses on attacking at all fronts, in the hopes that just one product out of many will become a certified hit, if it's fortunate enough to meet the needs of the customer at the right time.

Nevertheless, cut-and-paste marketing should be avoided at all costs. Consumers are savvy to corporate gimmicks that are solely bent on generating sales, which backfire in the form of a negative response. Companies that hastily try to parody a craze are sometimes slapped with copyright infringement lawsuits. Companies need to be aware of the fine line between enjoying the RC Ride with its customers and respecting boundaries within reason.

The RC Riders, Gen Z consumers who seek out hip spending opportunities, are setting today's trends. Roller Coasters may offer a thrilling diversion, but their operation depends on a strict observance of safety regulations. In other words, companies need to be held accountable for a certain level of risk in order to meet their customers' needs for thrilling diversions. As in the case of roller coasters at popular amusement parks, trendsetting companies need to install fail-safes so that their customers can thoroughly enjoy their products and services.

COWBOY HERO

YOUR DAILY SPORTY LIFE

Fitness is trending. Hiking trails are filled with young people sporting colorful leggings. Golf and surfing, once considered pastimes to a select few, are gaining a larger following. Running has evolved into trail runs and "clean sessions"; yoga now includes floating yoga, meditation yoga and sunset yoga. More importantly, the trend is not limited to the activity itself but has also become prevalent in fashion, selfies and social media challenges, positively influencing society overall and furthermore helping people realize their personal growth. Such enthusiasts have a strong tendency to expand their affinity for fitness through crews and communities.

The fitness trend is not simply a side effect of COVID-19 and the ensuing interest in boosting health and immunity. It is an amalgamation of Generation MZ's (millennials + Generation Z) affinity for self-management, the pursuit of a sense of accomplishment through exercise in an age of immobility, and market growth in hiking gear and fitness streaming platforms. Daily workouts indicate changes in the paradigm for everyday routines in the lives of consumers. Above all, as exercise becomes a part of one's daily routine, consumers will require brands to become "navigators" to support their leisure activity and "life activity designers" to help plan their overall

lifestyles. Daily workout routines demonstrate how Koreans' standards in life have shifted from success and competition to the pursuit of enjoyable and healthy values.

Colorful leggings that accentuate the curves, long fashion socks that fully cover the ankles, T-shirts emblazoned with giant-sized logos. Baseball caps and bucket hats, as well as fanny packs that complete the outfit. An endless line of youngsters parading in all shapes, colors and sizes. No, this is not the scene at a newly opened mall or hotspot. This is the scene in front of the Yeonjudae hermitage atop Mount Gwanak관악산, south of Seoul. Hiking trails have become as fashionable as catwalks. Hikers patiently wait in line to take a "proofie" in front of a boulder carved with the words: "Mt. Gwanak: 629 meters above sea-level."

One of the hotspots of today is the mountain. Millennials and hiking: the two may seem somewhat incongruous, but they have emerged together as a rising trend. Hiking has become an outdoor activity that the younger generation can easily take part in as a small group or even by oneself. Those dubbed "newbie hikers" tend to wear colorful leggings paired with long socks, and throw in bucket hats or baseball caps to complete the light hiking look. It's miles apart from the hiking uniforms of the older generation, armed with heavy trail boots, unvarying outdoor jackets, and long hiking sticks.

Hiking is emerging as a new workout trend among those in their 20s and 30s. Long considered an arduous activity shunned by many, it is now considered a fashionable pastime. Other activities that used to be exclusive to the older generation have become hip, and those that enjoy activities uncommon in the past are on the rise. Furthermore, one type of exercise can diverge, combine with, or evolve into other forms, as more people seek to expand their life experiences through exercise. Various pursuits have combined with workouts to expand the scope of sports activities.

An age of fitness emerges that incorporates exercise in everyday life, and in which workouts become daily routines and vice versa. This new cadre places exercise at the heart of their lifestyle, utilizing it as a means to define themselves, and enjoy their workouts to encourage a healthier self rather than embark on a spartan diet. We take a closer look at this new exercise trend, or "today's workout." Why has exercise become so trendy among Koreans, whose only strenuous workouts were back in gym class? We delve into the world of the latest workouts that have grabbed the attention of people living in the age of V-nomics (see chapter 1) whose hearts and minds have been battered by the "corona blues."

Taking a Look at the "Workout of the Day," #WOD

- *#hikestagram (hike + Instagram) #solohike and 3 million similar hashtags*
- *Number of surfers in Korea has exploded five-fold in the last five years*[1]
- *Percentage of golf course visitors among those born in the 1990s has jumped to 31.3 percent* [2]

Fitness is trending. For millennials, workouts have become a daily routine as well as a leisure activity, a hobby and a specialty. COVID-19 has resulted in a protracted period of social distancing, leading to more interest in safe exercises that minimize contact with strangers. Activity and hobby platforms have developed in line with such demands. Membership of the activity platform Frip프립, for example, has reached 950,000 as of June 2020. Its classes with the biggest following include hiking, surfing, freediving, kayaking, walking tours and fishing. So, why are hiking, surfing and freediving so popular among the myriad of sports activities? A rising interest in workouts does not necessarily mean all forms of exercise have become popular. What are trendsetters pursuing as their go-to workouts and how do they differ from existing exercises? What defines a "hip" sports activity?

What is interesting is not simply the increase in the

number of workout enthusiasts, but also the changes in the exercise culture led by those in their 20s and 30s. Cultural changes lead to an evolution in the landscape of related industries. Changes in exercise trends and related industries are transpiring not just in Korea but across the globe. The market cap for Shimano, a leading maker of cycling parts and gear in Japan, has bypassed that of car manufacturing giant Nissan. The total market cap for Lululemon Athletica, dubbed the "Chanel of yoga apparel," overtook that of Germany's BMW by $4 billion (as of August 2020). Lululemon achieved this explosive growth in less than a year: BMW's market cap exceeded that of Lululemon by $20 billion at the end of 2019.[3]

Such changes symbolize how exercise has broadened its definition from mental and physical training to incorporate a wider scope of experiences, self-realization and relationships, leading to an improved quality of life. An examination of the exercise lifestyle is becoming a barometer to infer how consumers spend their time, and a standard to predict key changes in the related industry.

I want to work out, but not just one workout – Diversifying the experience

"I do Pilates regularly on my own. I also swim, cycle and lift weights. Doing just one is too boring. Challenging myself to

take part in various sports helps invigorate my everyday life."

— A 26-year-old female office worker speaking at a focus group discussion (FGD) at the SNU Consumer Trend Center.

A distinct aspect of the daily workout is that consumers enjoy them in various forms and by various means. We find here two types: the first expands various types of workouts in a horizontal fashion, while the other diversifies one type of exercise into numerous vertical variations. The horizontal expansion refers to challenging oneself to take part in a wide range of activities, some of which may have been exclusive to different age groups or which may not have been popular before. The vertical variation refers to combining one's daily exercises with various other activities to seek newer experiences.

Case in point, those that enjoy hiking and golf are getting noticeably younger. Hiking in particular, a sport previously regarded as exclusive to the older generation, has become fashionable. In March 2020, the number of visitors to Mount Dobong도봉산 jumped 41.7 percent year on year.[4] A similar increase in the number of visitors to Mount Bukhan 북한산 in general was attributed to an increase of those in their 20s and 30s. Their varied approach to healthy hiking in proximity with nature has led to an influx of the younger demographic among hiking enthusiasts.

And as with the youthful revamp in the hiking demographic, there has been a similar revamp in mobile apps for newbie hikers. Tranggle트랭글 bestows 66 ranks on its users, starting from "Porter1" to "Heavenly Emperor7." Users can level up and receive rewards by completing missions as if playing a game, and even win online "badges" for completing a hiking trail. Ramblr램블러 provides detailed maps of ridges and specific names of locations on a trail or a mountain, and subdivides hiking trails under various themes. Every trail or route has a comment section in which users can write reviews upon completion, popular among newbie hikers seeking helpful tips for their upcoming trail. Millennials also organize "crews" through social media rather than join a mountaineering club. Hiking crews have a "founder" rather than a "leader" and hikes are more often dubbed "sessions." The number of new members on the Blackyak Alpine Club (BAC) app, sponsored by the mountain gear maker Blackyak doubled in April 2020, compared with a year earlier. Those in their 20s and 30s made up more than half of the new members. And in particular, the number of female members within that age bracket exceeded that of male members for the first time.[5]

Millennials are also fast emerging as major spenders in the world of golf. Online shopping mall operator Interpark reported a 62.5 percent jump in sales of golf-related goods in May and June, compared with a year earlier.[6] The Korea Golf Association reported that the number of Korean enthusiasts in their 20s and 30s make up 31.3 percent of the total, trailing only behind those in their 50s and 60s at 36.5 percent. In another survey, 56.6 percent of those in their 20s and 30s said they were interested in learning how to play golf.[7]

The influx of new golf consumers has also changed operations at country clubs. New clubs don't necessarily provide caddies and golf carts, in consideration of millennials who are more used to "untact" culture. Staff-less systems using electronic interfaces have become more common. The BlueOne Honors Country Club in Gyeongju, North Gyeongsang Province, offers smart check-in systems for solo rounds of golf, while the Lotte Skyhill Country Club in Jeju provides a self-payment counter, a computerized verification system, as well as a convenience store filled with vending machines.

New leisure activities that were previously uncommon are now drawing more enthusiasts. Water sports have been booming recently in Korea, with surfing emerging as a major summer activity. Every year some 100,000 visitors flock to Jukdo Beach in Yangyang, one of the nation's top three surfing spots, and even quite a few do so on weekdays. Freediving, once considered an unconventional activity exclusive to a select few, is also gaining a following. More people are signing up for one-day or long-term classes as the sport becomes more accessible.

The vertical variation adds diverse activities to a familiar

Young people flock to country clubs to play golf and enjoy surfing, once considered exclusive to a minority group.

workout routine and sets a new trend. For example, running can evolve into trail runs, and yoga into floating yoga, thus further adding to the appeal. Trail running combines hiking with running, and takes place in forests, on gravel and in other natural outdoor environments. The vigorous regimen requires the runner to dash quickly through various trails and courses, providing an effective workout while appreciating nature, and is popular among advanced sports enthusiasts seeking to intensify their routines. Night running, city runs and street runs that bypass hotspots and major landmarks are also variations on the common jogging and running routines.

Yoga has surprisingly evolved into floating yoga, sunset yoga, rooftop yoga, meditation yoga and other trendy variations. These vertical divergences break the monotony of the everyday routines and inject a much-needed source of inspiration.

Even with the same yoga postures, a different time and place will provide a unique experience. The hotel industry in particular has embraced the trend and is developing one-of-a-kind yoga programs. Shilla Hotel, for example, offers a floating yoga session at its swimming pool. Floating yoga burns more calories as it requires the yogi to execute their postures while finding their balance in the water. It's more popular in California, Hawaii and other areas where water leisure activities are more common. That's why the program provides phenomenal photo opportunities in which participants look as if they are in Hawaii or some other exotic location.

Meditation is also gaining popularity. There may be some contention as to whether meditation is an actual sport. Still, mediation as a form of exercise to "train the mind" is emerging as one of the top searches on mobile apps, YouTube, podcasts, and one-day classes. The trend is even more prevalent as the world continues to wait for a coronavirus vaccine. The mobile app Kokkiri코끼리, produced with the participation of a well-known Buddhist monk, the Venerable Haemin, is the country's largest meditation app. Mabo마보, another similar app, doubled its membership in a single month to 155,000 in April 2020.[6]

I want to work out, but not just work out - Expanding the self

Exercise can be defined as actions to train one's body and mind. However, consumers now seek more than just training through exercise. They want to record and prove their accomplishments. Another aspect of the daily workout is "expanding the self." Exercise is no longer limited to the actions themselves but becomes a means to express oneself and to reveal one's beliefs. The focal point of today's workout is not the type of exercise but whether it helps expand a sense of self. That is why you can't simply slap a "hip" hashtag on just any and every type of sport.

Take, for example, fashion, which helps express one's self. The newbie hikers rarely upload pictures of themselves wearing the usual hiking gear. Younger hikers' basic gear consists of colorful leggings, socks that cover the ankles, T-shirts with giant logos printed on the front, and windbreakers. Baseball caps, bucket hats and fanny packs accentuate the overall look. Such is their unbreakable fashion formula. They prefer minimal everyday clothing, and shy away from the tastes of the old guard, who more often sport high-tech clothing, heavy boots and mountaineering gear that seem more fitting for a climb up Mount Everest. This is the reason why the more traditional outdoor mountaineering clothing market remains in a slump even with the boom in the hiking population. Those that have maintained a line of clothing focused on costly high-functioning materials are losing their market share. Mammut, a Swiss maker of mountaineering and trekking gear, quietly closed its offices in 2020, and local clothing maker LF announced in 2019 that it was dropping its "Lafuma" outdoor clothing line.

Trendy hiking gear no longer looks like hiking gear. It's a fashion *faux pas* to wear clothing that screams "I'm going on a hike today!" A style that focuses on everyday wear, rather than the traditional outdoor sporting line, is what the industry dubs the "lifestyle concept" or "athleisure."

As a result, an outdoor brand's ability to meet the demand for lighter and simpler clothing that appeals to those in their 20s and 30s has become a make-or-break issue. Leggings are an example of hiking gear that doesn't look like hiking gear. The market for leggings has exploded because they can be worn for hiking, running, yoga and for other sports. Musinsa무신사, an online shopping mall operator, reported a sixfold increase in sales of sporting pants and leggings in the first half of 2020, compared with a year earlier.[7] That is more than double the increase in sales of sporting shirts and T-shirts. Sales of men's leggings have also jumped in line with the trend. Brands such as Andar and Xexymix that led the local leggings trend have revamped their line of men's shorts and leggings.

The "proofie" is also a crucial factor in the daily exercise routine. Classes accompanied by professional photographers are popular on activity platforms. GoPro video recordings are a must in freediving and paragliding sessions. This reflects a craving to capture their "pic of life인생샷" with the vast outdoors as the perfect backdrop. Solo trekkers often use mobile apps to navigate mountain trails. Hiking mobile app Relive lets the user edit photos into videos and upload them onto the app, sharing them with and receiving feedback from other users. An increasing number of people have "body profile" photos taken at professional studios, showing off the fruits of a spartan dietary and workout regimen. It's so popular that the number of posts with the tag #bodyprofile 바디프로필 has exceeded 1 million.[8]

Recording personal milestones is also necessary. Your sense of accomplishment is proportional to the number of goals you reach. Online workout mobile apps with LBS, or "location-based service," have long been leaders in the field. Nike Run Club (NRC) is one of the best known among such apps, with 107,371 monthly active users in April 2020, a year-on-year increase of 150 percent. Openrider, Strava, Adidas Runtastic, Relive and other apps with LBS features have also seen a jump in their membership from 52 percent to as much as 129 percent.[9]

The "Top 100 Mountain Hike Challenge" set by the Blackyak Alpine Club (BAC) app is renowned among enthusiasts. Hikers record and take photos at the mountain's summit and upload them onto the app to prove their climb.

Hence the long line to take pictures in front of the boulder at the Yeonjudae hermitage atop Mount Gwanak. It awards physical "patches" for each milestone of verified summits reached. Tranggle provides a record of every hiking session, similar to other running apps. At the end of a successful hike, the app awards hikers digital "badges," a reward system that further encourages a sense of accomplishment. Hikers even capture the screenshots of their patches and badges and upload them on social media, as if crossing out their "hiking bucket list."

The most recent trend combines trekking and hiking with nature conservation. "Plogging," originating from Sweden, where joggers pick up trash, "clean sessions" and "conscious trekking" which combine hiking and rubbish collecting, have been gaining popularity. Travelers are also gravitating toward backpacking that doesn't cause damage to nature and leaves a minimal carbon footprint. The trend reflects millennials' affinity for positive influences in their consumer habits. Uploads on BAC's "Clean Mountain 365" campaign have jumped 80 percent in May 2020 from a year earlier, and the number of first-time uploaders also jumped 63 percent in the same period. Posts with tags such as #cleanhiking and #trashtag are encouraging more to do their part in protecting the environment.

I want to work out, but not alone - Expanding relationships

The final aspect of the "today's workout" trend is "loose relationships." You don't want to work out alone, but nevertheless may find relationships a burden. You may want a pacemaker to run with you, but want to maintain a certain distance. "Separate but together" seems to be the latest trend in workout sessions. This would mean minimal after-workout dinners or separate social gatherings. On the odd occasion that you do take part in a social gathering, no one would force you to drink heavily. You can come and join or leave freely from the gathering. Going Dutch would be the rule of thumb. Workouts are no longer a solitary uphill battle. One can choose to enjoy sports together and expand relationships, while maintaining a comfortable emotional distance.

CrewGhost is one such social gathering that epitomizes a laid-back trend in running. It was founded in July 2016 with just two members and released its app in October of that year. The number of downloads surpassed 12,000 in 2019.[11] True to its name, runners join sessions and then part ways and disappear, like ghosts. Anyone can search for a running schedule and sign up on the app as they are all open sessions, suitable for the "today's workout" trends. In a similar vein, Nike has opened a web site called the "Nike Run Crew Finder" that lets users locate smaller running crews in their neighborhood. Crews can be browsed through according to their running method, crew type and location. Other sports are also leaning toward a crew support system. Sloth Climbing is the largest indoor and outdoor rock-climbing crew, active in Seoul and the surrounding Gyeonggi area. It provides an opportunity for those who are unsure about taking on rock climbing on their own to join sessions with other enthusiasts.

Relationships are not only expanding offline. More and more fitness buffs are working out at home as the pandemic has led to protracted lockdowns and social distancing measures. New York-based Peloton, dubbed "the Netflix of fitness," provides online fitness classes through a monthly subscription. Even though these online fitness classes mean its users are working out at home, Peloton's business concept, albeit contrary, is "connected fitness." When a member logs in to one of Peloton's channels, an instructor helps the member train in real time. Peloton showed steady growth even before the outbreak, but with the global lockdown, the number of members has soared exponentially. When asked about the key to Peloton's success, its CEO John Foley replied,

"The key was connection. We realized that by working out together, we can exercise longer, and make the experience more enjoyable. We wanted to give a sense of working out 'together' as a community even when working out at home."

Zwift, an online cycling and running program launched in 2015, has virtually created an online cycling and running community. It allows members to ride their bicycles while wearing smart trainers and Bluetooth earphones to enjoy virtual rides through London, New York City, Innsbruck and other virtual worlds, as part of a community. Members can link up with other users located across the globe to form teams and compete with one another.

Why Are Millennials So into Fitness?

Exercising has been a human activity for a long time. Defining "exercise" as a trend of 2021 is not just its linear extension. It is a culmination of the values held by millennials in their 30s and by Generation Z in their 20s, collectively known as "Generation MZ," as well as developments in the industry and technology, and of the unique set of circumstances precipitated by a global pandemic.

Youth does not belie complacency: generation MZ "saves up health" for a rainy day

A modern twist on a traditional idiom holds that "generosity comes from a (healthy) storehouse," meaning one can only afford to be affectionate with one's family or acquaintances, and magnanimous with oneself only with the support of a healthy body. Generation MZ doesn't put off until tomorrow whatever they want to do and whatever they need to do; they do it right away. They do not allow the workplace to encroach on their health, nor do they carelessly waste their youth. For them, exercising is akin to saving up for a rainy day. A wide variety of goals set by such individuals has helped expand the base for fitness regimens. For example, Generation MZ does not exercise simply to lose weight. A female comedian said recently on a TV program that she works out to eat whatever she wants, and to stay healthy. Many viewers who empathized with her voiced their support, illustrating this fitness trend.

When life doesn't turn out the way you planned: seeking self-esteem through accomplishment

Exercise is an important channel that allows a sense of accomplishment and confirms one's self-esteem. The sense of accomplishment feels more acute in a modern society that tends to hold back on praise and expressing satisfaction. Praise and compliments allow one to feel that "I'm alright." Weight management app Noom accentuates this point: Noom's management coaches never scold or point out members' mistakes. They continue to praise small accomplishments so that users are motivated to never give up midway and to ultimately reach their goal. A local sports brand representative holds a similar view. A workout lifestyle that young people want to adhere to cannot and should not be excessively arduous. Shorter running courses and simpler events allow participants to enjoy workouts as mini festivals. Any accomplishment, however small, can elevate a sense of self and provide motivation to stick to the workout regimen.

Fitness platforms that transcend space and time, and the growth of the related industry

The growth in exercise gear and platforms has played a major role in expanding fitness lifestyles among the general public. The market for wearable devices such as activity bands and smart watches is on the rise. Apple Watch is collaborating with Nike Run Club, while Samsung's Galaxy Watch is teaming up with Under Armour's Map My Run app to help users record and measure workouts, and even offer coaching advice. What's more notable is that the sports-related industry is quickly transforming itself into a service-oriented industry. Peloton's success in offering online fitness content has prompted similar service providers to jump on the bandwagon in the U.S market.

Mirror, which provides interactive home gym content using a digital mirror, is a piece of technology that has been grabbing consumers' attention. The user has access to streaming or video-on-demand workout content that includes muscular training, yoga, ballet, boxing and stretching, even allowing two-way communication with trainers.

Lululemon Athletica, which took note of Mirror's singular technology, acquired the company for $500 million. The field of sports will likely expand in line with advances in technology related to augmented reality (AR) and virtual reality (VR), even beyond the limitations of space and time.

Self-Preservation and Countermeasures Against COVID-19

The sports and fitness market saw steady growth, even before the outbreak of COVID-19. However, the pandemic has triggered an explosive interest in fitness and workouts. As the virus escalated and forced a prolonged lockdown around the world, consumer awareness for health has heightened. Their craving for leisure and outdoor activities, while still adhering to social distancing measures, has prompted interest in sports such as hiking and trekking. Analysts point out that while the pandemic has annihilated the travel industry, bookings for outdoor activities are still on the rise. COVID-19 has allowed us to focus on the more fundamental aspects of life, such as the family, nature and pre-digital, or "analog," sensitivities, thus leading to an explosive interest in exercises that fulfil the need for leisure activity while limiting physical contact. In the age of the New Normal, workouts have become a means for physical health and mental stability removed from the hustle and bustle of city life, as well as a most cost-effective investment.

Outlook and Implications

— Being a Life Designer to Build a Healthier Lifestyle

The sports of today have expanded into our daily routines and evolved into enjoyable activities, rather than stagnating as simple matches to determine wins and losses. More than six out of ten people in their 20s and 30s take part in regular exercise at least once a week, according to a 2019 report by the Ministry of Culture, Sports and Tourism. So, what kind of changes can we expect when routines become workouts and vice versa?

The trend will likely continue to blur the lines between daily clothing and sportswear. More consumers will opt for lighter sports gear that can be worn as everyday clothing, shying away from heavier and more professional lines. Three out of ten people bought athleisure gear, and eight out of ten showed interest in wearing such clothing, according to research company Macromill Embrain's survey of 1,000 people. Only 13 percent of the respondents said they only wear athleisure clothing during workouts.

The prevalence of the coronavirus has fanned the need for "one-mile wear," or clothing that can be worn within a one-mile (1.6 kilometer) radius of one's home, including clothing suitable for workouts and visits to the neighborhood supermarket. In other words, the sports gear of today has to be functional and versatile as well as activity-friendly.

The New Normal of social distancing has given rise to wellness and mindfulness tours that emphasize self-development, such as meditation and yoga.

Jogger pants and activity-friendly underwear are fast emerging as the latest fashion trend, even more so than leggings. Outdoor sports brands that placed heavier emphasis on functionality now face a fork in the road: to change or not to change.

Travel and hotel industries, decimated by the impact of COVID-19, will likely be able to find a way out of the crisis by offering leisure programs focusing on sports and activities. Hotels and tourist destinations were starting to incorporate such leisure activities even before the spread of the virus. This would appeal to millennials who value varied experiences. According to a travel report by Hotels.com, 93 percent of millennials were interested in bold self-development in their travel choices. Such characteristics are prevalent among those who seek travel that encourage physical and mental development through learning and experiencing something new. Wellness tourism and mindfulness tours are emerging as the latest trend in the industry. According to a Global Wellness Institute report, the wellness tourism market will likely expand to $919 billion in 2022 from $639 billion in 2017.[12] Korea will likely reflect such global trends as consumers adhere to social distancing measures and opt for tours that provide a wide variety of activities and experiences, including meditation and yoga.

Sports brands will likely take on a stronger role as lifestyle designers, as the realm of workouts slowly seep into consumers' everyday routines. The average consumer does not want to become an expert in a specified sports field. They want to capture a myriad of brilliant moments to complete a chapter in their lives. Therefore, corporations will be required to play the role of "navigator" and "life activity designer" that supports consumers' leisure lives.

More people are incorporating exercise as part of their daily routines, in line with a shift in life standards from success and competition to the pursuit of enjoyable and healthy values. In the end, companies that reflect such values will be the ones left standing. The winners will become life designers to consumers, already exhausted physically and mentally from the pandemic, paving the way for a healthier lifestyle.

COWBOY HERO

HEADING TO THE RESALE MARKET

Today's market for previously owned items is in a different league from that of the past. Rather than scorned as castoffs, they are appreciated almost as much as brand-new products, no matter how many times they change hands. We would like to call these goods "Nth New Products," referring to a trend that values repurchased items, no matter how many owners have preceded them. Nth New Products are also viewed as an up-and-coming tool for financial management. This includes earning extra cash by selling items that one does not use anymore, or even selling one's particular talents. "Resales" of luxury goods or limited-edition sneakers at a premium, has become a new means of investment for Generation MZ. Trading platforms for secondhand goods have emerged as a new consumer playground.

The secondhand market is also acting as a medium that brings people together as a community. It is evolving into a lifestyle platform with secondhand enthusiasts banding together by their local residential areas. The key reason for its explosive growth can be attributed to today's emphasis on eco-conservation, Gen MZ's propensity to be generous (yet quickly bored) with sharing, the rise of frugal financial management and stuck-at-home spending, and the development of secure and user-friendly trading platforms.

In order for the market to take root, its services and related regulations need to be strengthened to enhance transparency and reliability. As such, companies need to become more flexible in their approach, embracing consumers who are enthusiastic about the secondhand market. Nth New Products no longer mean "old and worn inferior goods." The market needs to respond to the needs of consumers who find Nth New Products more appealing than brand-new merchandise.

#1 A young professional with 2 million won spends 1 million won on a laptop. How much does he believe he has left? The answer is not 1 million won, but 1.4 million won. He can always resell the laptop and get 400,000 won.

#2 *"I bought a pre-owned million-won Kurzweil SP4-8 for 700,000 won, and had fun playing it for six months. I resold it for 600,000. That means I got to use it for six months for 100,000 won."* [1]

Generation MZ differs from older generations in many ways, but there is one aspect that stands out: their attitude towards trading used goods. For most members of the older generations, who did not come from a privileged background, "pre-owned" goods held negative connotations, implying "castoffs" or "hand-me-downs." Secondhand goods were a symbol of poverty, the only alternative when one could not afford a brand-new product. To Gen MZ, however, the pre-owned market becomes a means for a valuable purchase at a reasonable price, an investment tool, a playground for scavenger hunts and for trading according to one's preferences, as well as a space that connects people. How well one makes use of the secondhand market has become a new standard for being "hip."

Today's market for secondhand products is estimated at 20 trillion won ($17.5 billion). It has become even hotter than the primary market which deals in new merchandise. According to a report on the "Analysis of the Secondhand Goods App Market" by Mobile Index, a mobile data analysis platform, daily users of the secondhand trading app Daangn당근마켓 reached 1.56 million, second only to the nation's favorite shopping app, Coupang쿠팡 with 3.97 million. Daangn not only beat giant online shopping malls such as 11Street, Gmarket, WeMakePrice and TMON, but it was also the only secondhand trading app among the top five shopping apps in Korea.[2] This frenzy over trading in pre-owned goods is slowly spreading beyond Gen MZ.

We would like to take a closer look at this market for pre-owned merchandise from various angles. Secondhand goods are no longer just "items previously owned by someone else." Even after changing hands multiple times, they can hold as much value as brand-new products. As such, we would like to define them as "Nth New Products." It signifies a trend that sees used products as new, despite trading them for the umpteenth time. The term "resale," or "resell," is also more widely used to indicate investment-type trades in which previously owned items are sold at a premium. As consumers chase after N^{th} New Products that they consider more appealing and valuable than brand-new merchandise, we take a look at how this trend will likely affect the market in the future.

The Nth New Product: A New Paradigm is Born

"I wired the money. Is shipping included?"
"Excuse me, but are you RM from BTS? The name and address seem right [...]"
"Thank you." [3]

This is part of a text message exchange that spread like fire through the online community. A reseller shared screenshots from his phone after he sold a pair of secondhand trousers. What caught people's attention was that the leader of the world's most famous boyband BTS not only traded in used products, but that he also cares about shipping costs. And he is not alone. Online communities often cite stories about celebrities who have taken to trading in secondhand goods.

The rise of Nth New Products does not only indicate an expansion of the market for previously owned items, but also represents a fundamental change in perception. It is a far different matter from the trade in secondhand goods during the 1997 Asian financial crisis as part of a campaign to conserve, share, exchange, and reuse goods. N^{th} New Products are changing consumer paradigms in two major ways.

First, the myth surrounding brand-new products is crumbling. Secondhand goods are not alternatives chosen when new merchandise is unaffordable. Consumers no longer have misgivings about previously used items, but consider them to be perfectly serviceable, reasonably priced and cost effective. Gen MZ, the movers and shakers of the secondhand market, are a "Money-friendly Generation," familiar from an early age with an abundance of brands and products. The growth of the market has produced goods that are nearly indistinguishable from one another, prompting this generation to put less weight on brand-new merchandise. This Money-friendly Generation is well aware that all new products inevitably become secondhand goods and does not obsess over shiny new commodities. Secondly, the growth of the pre-owned market indicates that consumer focus has shifted from "possession" to "actual use" of the product. Aficionados declare that it is better to buy a 300,000-won ($262) shirt, wear it five times and then resell it for 200,000 won, rather than purchase a 100,000-won shirt, wear it 10 times and throw it into the wardrobe, never to be seen again. They would rather have the experience of wearing clothes worth 300,000 won than owning clothes worth 100,000 won. Gen MZ adapts to everchanging trends and enjoys exposure to new stimulation in order to discover their identity and self-worth. What is more important for them is the experience of discovering hip and rare items, rather than owning new products. Once the experience is over, they resell or donate them instead of stockpiling items they don't really need at home. As such, secondhand goods are not thrown away but are relisted as available goods and compete shoulder-to-shoulder with new products. In other words, the growth of Nth New Products is a shift towards a cyclical consumer trend that flows from purchase to disposal and back to repurchase.

The growth of the market for secondhand goods is a precursor to a paradigm shift in consumer patterns. We stand at a crossroad of great transformation. This is the reason we need to take a closer look at changes to the consumer landscape brought on by N^{th} New Products.

Gen MZ may have triggered changes in the secondhand market, but the trend seems to be spreading to the older generations as well. According to a *Chosun Ilbo* survey of 1,535 men and women ranging from their 20s to 60s, the age groups who most actively traded in previously owned goods were those in their 30s (65.4%) and 40s (60.8%). Even those in their 50s and 60s are also increasing their presence in the market as they make more use of their smartphones due to COVID-19 and social distancing. More

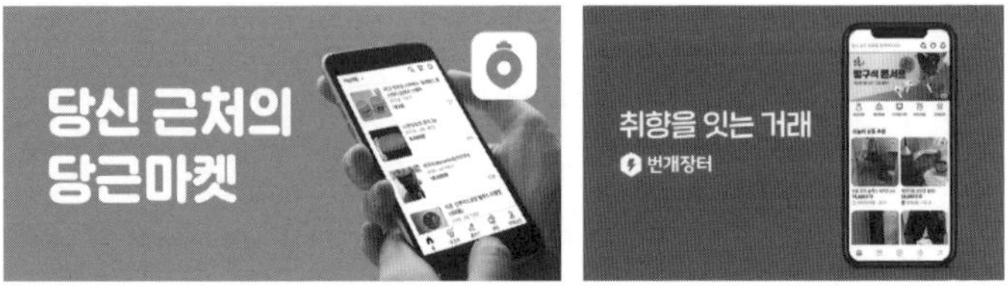

Daangn당근마켓 and Bungaejangter번개장터, the nation's top thrift platforms. Daangn's average daily users stand at 1.6 million, and is the No. 2 shopping app in Korea.

and more among the older generations have left comments saying they are taking their cue from their children reselling possessions online to make some quick cash.

Online secondhand trading platforms are also transforming in various ways. The aforementioned Daangn is the mobile app receiving the most attention so far, with its humble beginnings in 2015 when it was the Gyeonggi Province-based "Pangyo Marketplace판교장터." It adopted its current name in October of the same year and began its nationwide service in January 2018. "Daangn," which on its own means "carrot" in Korean, is actually an acronym for "your당신 neighborhood근처 market," in which a deal is only possible within a six-kilometer radius of your location. The app has seen triple growth in the past year as region-based trades proved reliable and continued to grow. Its users showed average daily usage of 20 minutes and 24 log-ons per month, with total app downloads reaching 20 million. As the service has entered the vernacular, if you are "Daangning" an item, you are putting your possession up for sale. And with many users buying and then reselling an item multiple times on Daangn (often called "re-Daangning"), buyers would sometimes ask how many Daangns the item has been through.

There are platforms that have an even narrower radius. Market Village마켓빌리지 restricts deals to within a one-kilometer radius. It provides a differentiated service of limiting deals to within the same apartment complex, or residential area. Everytime에브리타임 is the equivalent of Daangn among college students. It is better known as an online student community platform, but its bookstore category shows active trade in secondhand textbooks and teaching materials.

Secondhand trading platforms are also evolving to specialize in specific items. ThankQMarket땡큐마켓, dealing in children's goods; Feelway필웨이, focusing on luxury brands, Golmarket골마켓, dedicated to golf-related products; and Mule뮬, an indispensable trading site for musicians, all deal with previously owned commodities. Experimental startups such as Parabara파라바라 are also noteworthy. It introduced unmanned vending machines for secondhand goods. Products for sale are placed in a transparent locker, along with contact details, product description and a price estimate, enabling "untact" trades. The first vending machine was placed at the Junggye branch of Lotte Mart in northeastern Seoul in August 2020, and plans for installing additional units in Gwanggyo and Yangpyeong in Gyeonggi Provincc are under review. As reselling becomes a more central feature of consumer behavior, we expect even more platforms and services to flood the market in line with the trend.

The products listed on these platforms are sometimes mind-boggling. A tin of Lemona Vitamin C powder, emblazoned with the face of BTS member Jungkook, goes for 30,000 won ($26) An empty bottle of Chanel perfume is listed at 20,000 won ($17.50). An Hermes shopping bag is priced at 15,000 won ($13). Though you may wonder who would want to pay good money for such items, they are, surprisingly or not, sought after items in the secondhand market. The market for Nth New Products is transforming into an arena for trading never before seen unique items, in addition to the usual fare of secondhand goods. Retro items are also coveted in the market. The No. 1 search word in the books and hobbies section on second-hand platform Bungaejangter번개장터 (meaning "lightning marketplace") in the first-half of 2020 was "My Melody," a character created by Japan's Sanrio in the 1970s. Retro coffee cups and mugs, as well as vintage dishware, are favorites among customers who favor Nth New Products.[4]

Daangn also regularly features local favorites and specialties. Densely populated areas such as Seongnam, Bundang and Suji in Yongin, see heavy trade in children's goods, while Jeju Island's listings feature freshly caught seafood such as top shells and red stingrays. Areas with a large number of single-person households even have half-used bottles of shampoo for sale. Uncommon items such as bricks and soil, as well as camping gear and even country homes, are also listed for sale.

Every Sale Ends in Payment: the Nth New Investment Technique

"If you're lucky, you can score a pair of limited-edition kicks on a resale app. If its market value goes up, you can turn a tidy profit by reselling them again on the same app." [5]

Trading in secondhand goods is fast emerging as a new investment technique, going beyond the usual means of making some money on the side. The market has become a handy way to earn money for a lot of Gen MZers who lost part-time or regular jobs due to the protracted period of social distancing. The most active trades involve fanboying or fangirling hobbies, called "deokjil덕질." Trades are not limited to goods, but can also include talents and specialties, such as illustrations of one's favorite characters, images, pet portraits, or even stickers to decorate portfolios and journals. These are listings for "commissions," in which one's talents or labor are put up for sale. Bungaejangter, the platform favored by teenagers and those in their 20s, has a high number of "commission" listings. One's special skills and talents become marketable.

The older generations are also getting involved by selling "old" items. With the outbreak of the pandemic, they are left with free time to reorganize their belongings, putting some of their possessions up for sale on the market. Clothing that took up space in their wardrobe, kitchen appliances that gathered dust in the corner, and seldom-used furniture are all appearing on the listings. Even large and bulky items are put up for resale as it is more profitable – and sometimes easier – than trying to dispose of them. More and more are discovering the joy of reselling rather than purchasing. Some have even taken to selling secondhand goods at a premium. As mentioned earlier, a "resale" often refers to selling rare items at a premium. Its common definition is the sale of pre-owned items, but recently it has been used to describe the sale of luxury or limited-edition goods at a profit.

In the summer of 2020, a customer ordered 300 cups of coffee at a Starbucks to receive the promotional Summer Ready Bags and Summer Chairs, taking just one cup and leaving the remaining 299 cups behind.[6] Some may think that this is a waste, but if the customer sells the promotional items on a resale platform, he or she can make a profit of 30,000 to 50,000 won ($26-$44) per item. These unique Starbucks goods were indeed heavily sought after on resale apps. According to Bungaejangter's analysis of its trading data between May 1 and August 22, the No. 1 item was the Starbucks Summer Ready Bag. The words "Ready Bag" appeared in 250,000 searches and resulted in an estimated 2,500 successful deals.[7]

The appeal of limited editions has turned Nth New Products into a viable form of investment. In May 2020, rumors that Chanel would raise prices prompted long queues in front of department stores before opening hours that led to stampedes, which was all the more alarming due to social distancing concerns at the time. The main reason for the opening-hour rush, or "open run" as they are called, was of course the profit margin related to what's known as a "Chanel investment." The price for a medium-sized Chanel classic flap bag, which stood at 7.15 million won ($6,256) in May 2020, jumped to between 8.6 million and 9 million won by August on Joonggonara중고나라, a secondhand goods trading website. If a person succeeded in scoring the bag during the stampede, he or she would have pocketed a profit of 25.8 percent.[8]

Consequently, resales are an investment tool for Gen MZ. Resales of men's sneakers on Bungaejangter jumped 75.9 percent in 2020 from the previous year.[9] In November 2019, hopeful buyers lined up in an endless queue in front of Nike's Hongdae branch for the release of Air Force 1 "Para Noise" sneakers, a limited-edition collaboration between the sports brand and Korean singer G-Dragon. What was as-

Nike's limited-edition Air Force 1 "Para Noise." A pair of the 219,000 won sneakers are listed at 500,000 won in the resale market, and a pair autographed by K-pop sensation G-Dragon has a price tag of 15 million won.

tonishing was that the line was not for purchasing the kicks, but rather to obtain a raffle ticket that would randomly determine the lucky buyers. Among them, only 8,888 hopeful buyers, wearing the requisite Nike T-shirts and Air Force 1 sneakers, were awarded raffle tickets. And that's not all: that same evening, Joonggonara was filled with resale listings for the products at 500,000 won per pair, more than double the initial store price of 219,000 won. A pair with G-Dragon's autograph was listed at 15 million won.[10] Nike's May 2020 limited-edition collaboration with Ben & Jerry's, the SB Dunk Low "Chunky Dunky," which was initially sold for 129,000 won, saw its price hover between 1.3 million and 1.8 million won by July on Joonggonara. The seller would have made a more than tenfold profit in just two months.

In fact, the market for investing in shoes and sneakers is continually expanding. Those hoping to buy rare items are all too eager to camp out for days in front of the stores to buy limited editions. The cutthroat competition has also led to changes in sales methods. Retailers have adopted the raffle system, breaking away from the conventional first-come, first-served format. The raffle system ensures equitability and generates more publicity. A limited release sale in a raffle scheme is cause for considerable hype among Gen MZers. Expectations of as yet unannounced raffles prompt frequent visits to retailers' websites and mobile apps.

The growth of the resale market has prompted corporations to get in on the action. Search engine giant Naver's image and video messaging app SNOW launched its sneaker resale platform "KREAM," and shopping platform Musinsa opened its own resale platform "Soldout." Larger conglomerates are also jumping on the bandwagon. Lotte Shopping joined hands with the nation's first sneaker resale platform "Out of Stock" for its foray into the market.

Staying Up Until the Wee Hours: the Nth New Playground

Trading secondhand items has become a pastime, providing a source of entertainment and emotional satisfaction. The seller plays the roles of promoter and salesperson, while the buyer gets to enjoy the back-and-forth exchange of the bargaining process. Copywriting an ad for a pre-owned item becomes a stimulating creative test of one's wits. When writing an ad for a leftover length of rope, a seller adds a tag: "Don't tie yourself in knots." When writing about a rare 1972 coin, another seller adds a tag to entice people born in the 70s. Sellers can also "curate" their own packages. The increase in single-person households has prompted sellers to offer, for example, a set of daily necessities, or pairing a book with an LP record, targeting those living alone. An unconventional offering can also draw buyers' attention. Sellers often use self-taught sales skills to pique the shopper's interest, such as pairing a spring/autumn jacket with a can of whelks, often a favorite during the cooler seasons. Buyers also enjoy the process of negotiation. Fierce bargaining may be frowned upon, but a light tug-of-war provides delightful amusement and memories of friendly haggling in traditional markets.

In fact, the appeal of trading secondhand goods stems from the element of surprise. The anticipation of discovering a gem hidden among the clutter adds to the allure of the secondhand market. Such expectations carry over to online platforms. To Gen MZ, these markets are a treasure trove. Even when they don't need anything in particular, they open their app and browse through the listings as a force of habit. As mentioned, Daangn's report shows that the average user visits more than 20 times a day. They visit and swipe through the listings as if browsing through their social media feeds of friends and associates with shared interests. Such "Instagram-style" browsing is applied to platforms for pre-owned goods. These consumer patterns imply that the market is not just a place to buy and sell merchandise, but also a means of leisure. The act of purchasing is not simply born out of necessity: visiting online shopping sites like an explorer in the jungle is a type of "fauxsumerism," where users derive satisfaction from browsing, creating wish lists or filling their online shopping carts without making an actual purchase. This can also be called "exploratory consumer buying behavior." On the flipside, "purposeful buying behavior" stems from necessity. Experts point out that the exploratory shopper experiences a sense of competence from the process of browsing and discovering rare finds in secondhand markets.[11] Early online malls focused on purposeful shopping patterns, as they provided instant information on where to find the best deals for the item in question. The secondhand market, on the other hand, is a brave new world. Consumer patterns are shifting towards the joy of unearthing a diamond in the rough. It also becomes a test of one's skill to identify underrated items.

More Chat than Trade: Sharing N^th^ New Products

Personal tastes are like alter egos for Gen MZ, and are powerful ways to express oneself. As such, Gen MZ flock together in like-minded swarms within the secondhand trading market. Bungaejangter, popular among those in their teens and 20s, offer diverse content for their target consumers. Their weekly campaign of "Trading According to Tastes" held every Friday is one such example. "Finding the Right Camping Chair" for camping newbies, and "Must-haves for an At-Home Concert" for K-pop fans, or "Top 5 Biker Items" for motorcycle enthusiasts, bring together sellers of items that suit the specified tastes of particular buyers. This is the biggest advantage of Nth New Products: bringing together buyers and sellers with similar tastes.

These people with shared interests often talk shop, sharing tips, information, and step-by-step instructions on the use of particular items. This includes rooting for the buyer's future level-ups while selling a PlayStation game, or making friends through frequent trades of rare LPs. Buying secondhand items on these platforms often leads to the rare chance of obtaining an expanded set of related items. Browsing the listings for a DSLR camera often can yield results that include a lens or a tripod. One can find complete or specifically curated sets of all manner of collectibles sold by collectors and enthusiasts.

Personal tastes also help eliminate the risk of uncertainty in the secondhand market. One major difference of the online platforms of today is that the potential buyer can now check up on previous sales records of the seller. The buyer can see what kind of goods the seller has previously sold and confirm his or her tastes and interests. Rather than concentrating on the price tag, the buyer can establish trust with the seller through a common interest, ultimately "following" the seller and his listings.

A closer proximity adds to the sense of reliability in trading items that represent shared tastes. Daangn's success was not only the convenience of trading among people within a limited area. Every district has its local flavor, and these trades would reflect such unique characteristics. As a result, Daangn remains a largely community-based trading platform. In truth, there are stories of trades leading to friendships, and even a heartwarming tale of reuniting with a lost dog through the Daangn platform.

Locally based secondhand trading platforms are evolving into online communities to share information about the neighborhood. When Daangn started discovering listings for local classes and lectures, the platform launched a separate "Village Life동네생활" service to share local information, expanding the service nationwide in September 2020 as "In My Neighborhood내 근처" which brought small businesses and local residents together. What is more interesting is that Daangn changed its app category from "Shopping" to "Social." Such transformation brings to mind the evolution of San Francisco-based Craigslist, which had its humble beginnings as a newsletter containing local classified ads, and is currently a nationwide community platform providing a multitude of services ranging from job searches, to information on hobby groups, to real estate listings.

Background: Changing the Production & Consumer Paradigm

Dealing in secondhand items, one of the oldest forms of trade, is changing the paradigm of manufacturing and consumption, and is impacting our daily lives more than ever before. So why have Nth New Products emerged as a hot commodity, overtaking brand-new merchandise?

The eco-friendly generation's concern over disposal

Environmental conservation is a primary concern for Gen MZ. Climate change concerns and a global viral outbreak have triggered these eco-friendly traits, with considerations on how best to put into practice the appropriate disposal of goods. Nth New Products meets this consumer perspective, as they provide an alternative to buying new merchandise by reusing items that aren't needed by others. ThredUp, the largest U.S. online thrift store, asserted that the secondhand market will outpace the size of fast fashion within 10 years. It also predicted that secondhand clothing will make up one third of a person's wardrobe by 2033.[12] Avid users of Daangn also point out that community-based face-to-face trading eliminates unnecessary waste and packaging.

Generous sharing vs. bored of sharing: the whims of Gen MZ

Changes in preconceptions about previously owned items have also added to the appeal of Nth New Products. The younger generation, now well-versed in the economics of sharing through Socar쏘카, Uber, Airbnb and WeWork, are no longer averse to buying secondhand goods. Members of Gen MZ also prefer pre-owned items because they can buy, use, and then resell them in keeping with fast-changing trends. They are always on the lookout for rare items, focusing on the experience of use rather than possession, taking proofies with the items, uploading them on social media, and then reselling them to others. To the older generations, their younger counterparts may seem fickle as they rarely hold on to an item for a considerable length of time. However, their solution to overcome boredom is to repeatedly buy and sell N^th^ New Products, which has contributed to this trend's rise.

The unrestricted feast of limited-release marketing

Limited-edition brand marketing has also added to the frenzy of the resale market. Collaborations with influencers on social media have been all the rage in marketing across all sectors in recent years. The pandemic has pushed businesses to boost marketing centered on limited releases as a means to bounce back from the economic slump. Limited editions are the "best bling" for Gen MZ to upload as proofies on social media. Luxury and sneaker brands in particular have adopted this format to generate hype, with the success of collaborative projects becoming a new measure of brand recognition. In other words, they have to design products that are "flex"-worthy. Analysts point out that Gen MZ's strong sense of self, as well as marketing strategies by brands to generate hype, have helped boost the resale market.

Scrimping through COVID-19: Soaring at-home purchases

The economic downturn has been a major factor in the surge of Nth New Products. The seller gets to list possessions gathering dust at home to make some extra cash. The buyer can sift through listings to obtain products at a fraction of their original price. Frugal money management, or the "Scrooge method" (known in Korea as *jjantech*짠테크, a neologism combining "cheap" and "technique"), such as selling gift vouchers and discount coupons issued by mobile phone companies, are often among the listings on college community platform "Everytime." A listing for four slices of pizza on Daangn once made headlines. The seller could not finish almost half the order of pizza and put it up for sale for 2,000 won ($1.75), striking a deal within two hours.[13] Stuck-at-home purchases amid the pandemic have also contributed to the rise of Nth New Products. People have been reorganizing their homes as they've become multipurpose areas, alternating from office, classroom to private space. They then list the items found in the process on to the thrift platform for sale.

Development of secure and user-friendly platforms

The development of mobile thrift platform apps breathed new life into the secondhand market. Platforms with simple and user-friendly interfaces lowered the barrier for many users who believed that secondhand trading was complicated. For example, Daangn eliminated a complicated registration process, allowing access to a wider age bracket. Face-to-face trading within a limited area also provided a sense of reliability and eased any burden for many users. These platforms also strived to minimize risk factors involved in trading secondhand goods and helped to expand the base for N^{th} New Products. The market had been limited by dormant risk factors such as fraud or lack of information, and the platforms took steps to rectify these flaws. The system is not quite perfect, but the operators are introducing policies aimed at establishing trust and reducing disputes among its users.

One such example is Daangn's "etiquette barometer," in which buyers rate sellers with positive or negative feedback that affects their rating, an important indicator for potential buyers. Bungaejangter introduced "Bungae Pay," an escrow-based secure payment service, in which the buyer deposits money into an escrow account and the seller receives it upon delivery of the goods, providing added security and eliminating concerns about possible fraud.

Outlook and Implications

— Revival of the Resale Market

The key to sustainable growth in the secondhand market lies in the level of confidence it generates among users through transparent trading. The issue of fraud inevitably creeps up as almost all trade in the market is a person-to-person exchange. A listing for earbuds sometimes results in a delivery of apples, or buying a laptop ends up with a delivery of bricks. According to the Korean National Police Agency, fraud cases involving online secondhand trading sites reached 136,074 in 2019, up 21.5 percent from the previous year.[14] Tax evasion is also a major concern. According to the Electronics Transactions Act, if trades exceed 20 cases within six months, and involve a total sum exceeding 12 million won ($10,500), the seller is obligated to pay a business income tax and a value-added tax. However, private trading through social media or private feeds are still blind spots for tax regulations.

Voluntary efforts within the market to secure confidence would be more effective than government crackdowns and regulations. Guarantees regarding the resale of valuable luxury goods and limited releases in particular will likely emerge as a major issue in the future. The growth of online thrift stores in the U.S. was led by platforms that offered money-back guarantees. The RealReal, an online used luxury goods retailer, verifies the authenticity of an item sent by the seller before listing the item. It has more than 100 experts on its inspection team to ensure a secure authentication process. This is particularly important for trades in luxury items that fetch large sums of money. Such efforts helped the company to be listed on NASDAQ in 2019, and it opened its 8,000 square-foot flagship store in San Francisco's Union Square in February 2020.

Used goods also include genuine products

Domestic platforms are also taking similar cues. Frog프로그, a resale platform for limited-edition footwear, launched its authentication service in August 2020. In order to alleviate buyers' concerns, Frog inspects the product and even provides a tag and a certificate of authentication, regardless of whether a deal takes place. Naver unit SNOW's KREAM, the online resale platform for sneakers, also beefed up its authentication process. Its team of experts carefully inspect goods according to authenticity, packaging, tags, as well as dirt and other defects, and only ship goods that pass muster.

And lastly, we can expect online resale market platforms to diversify and differentiate themselves by using AI and big data. Advances in machine learning will allow platforms to identify fake goods and remove them from their lists altogether. Thrift platforms will be able to automatically exclude listings of alcohol and tobacco items, which are prohibited from e-commerce. In August 2019, Bungaejangter acquired Voost부스트, a startup specializing in big data analysis, a cornerstone in Bungaejangter's plans to enhance user experience (UX) by augmenting its keyword searches, recommendations, and data mining through Voost's analysis and technology.

Society also needs to reach a consensus on irregular trading activities. Frankly speaking, reselling items at a premium can be construed as an illegal transaction. The prime example is a no tolerance policy against ticket scalping for movies, concerts and sporting events. Scalping has long been a topic of criticism, with numerous lawmakers proposing bills against such irregular trade. However, regulations against the resale of limited-edition sneakers and rare items at a premium is still somewhat vague. Unlike ticket resales, in which scalpers buy tickets in bulk, thereby snatching away the opportunity for others to enjoy the performance at the original price, the purchase of a limited-release pair of sneakers is a result of a person's valuable time and hard work. There are even those who place value on the skill of recognizing underrated items. Lee Eun-hee, a professor of consumer studies at Inha University in Incheon, said that if a person invested time and money to obtain a rare item on behalf of another person, then the value of that time and money spent in the process needs to be included in the adjusted price of the product.[15]

Can brand-new merchandise survive in a world of Nth New Products?

So, amid such changing trends in the market, manufacturers are left with the dilemma: How can their brand-new products survive in a world of Nth New Products? Experts say producers need to take into account that their brands may later be traded as secondhand goods. With Gen MZ embracing N^{th} New Products as a facet of the hip consumer lifestyle, so too should manufactures accept the trend as a preference held by younger generations. Galeries Lafayette, an upmarket French department store chain, collaborated with a Paris startup in April 2019 to launch "Le Good Dressing," an online resale platform for secondhand clothing. Unlike existing thrift store platforms, Le Good Dressing requires both the buyer and seller to physically visit the department store to complete the trade. Galeries Lafayette then rewards the seller with the store's gift voucher, ensuring that the proceeds return as future revenue.

Even luxury goods manufacturers that frowned upon The RealReal are slowly approaching the online luxury goods resale platform for possible collaboration. Stella McCartney agreed to offer $100 vouchers to customers who purchase

Trade of second-hand goods is fast becoming an industry trend that even leading brands and manufacturers can no longer ignore. IKEA introduced a buyback-service, through which customers can sell IKEA furniture back to the store.

her products on The RealReal. This is making use of a resale platform to convey a message to its clients: "Our brand strives for sustainability." Domestic stores are also taking similar steps. IKEA Korea's buyback-service, which was first launched at its Gwangmyeong store in July 2020, offered its customers a chance to sell the store's products back to IKEA. The company then repairs and restores the items and places them for resale to other customers. This reflects the needs of Gen MZers who spurn the fast fashion consumer trend (that exists even for furniture) of easily buying and then discarding furniture after one season. CNP Company, a restaurant and bakery franchise operator, supports an offline secondhand trading delivery platform for its "Nice Weather" convenience stores. In other words, it is offering delivery and pickup services for trading secondhand goods, the same way other convenience stores do with their regular package delivery systems. It also reflects its customers' concerns for the environment by donating part of their proceeds to international organizations that combat climate change.

The secondhand market is no longer a dumping ground for worn and inferior goods. The market paradigm is shifting to match consumer trends that favor discovering one's own "Nth value" rather than becoming the first owner of a brand-new product. Possibilities are boundless for Nth New Products, which repeatedly become brand-new items to someone somewhere. The market needs to address the needs of these consumer trends.

COWBOY HERO

EVERYONE MATTERS IN THE 'CX UNIVERSE'

Brand loyalty is waning amid an influx of available goods and related information. So how can one manage brands and succeed in digital transformation (DT) to meet the needs of consumers who seek convenience? The answer would be overall management of the customer experience, or "CX." When CX goes beyond simply managing consumer touchpoints and becomes an appreciation of the philosophy behind a specific brand, à la Marvel Cinematic Universe (MCU), we classify this as a "CX Universe."

Today's consumers cope with innumerable points of digital contact in which they seek a seamless experience free from conflict or hassle. As Generation MZ embraces experiential marketing, an increasing number of companies feel the need to prioritize a unique CX as part of their competitive strategy, enhancing how they provide such experiences to their customers. Creating a CX Universe requires companies to: (1) Provide a seamlessly smooth experience; (2) Induce customers to freely share data about their experiences; and (3) Provide them with a novel and interesting experience. Organizations currently undertaking digital transformation should focus on an overall enhancement of the customer experience. CX is a road that winds through trust and immersion towards loyalty. This road does not simply end there but loops back for the next purchase. This process becomes ever more steadfast in a repetitive sequence called the "CX Cycle."

In an age of waning brand loyalty, the "CX Cycle" has become the goose that lays the golden egg. Companies striving to create fandoms like those of the MCU and to allow customers to enjoy the expanding of the universe they want with their brand, should herald 2021 as the dawn of CX innovation.

As the saying goes, "You can find a Starbucks on every corner," especially in the Gangnam area in southern Seoul, all of which are jam-packed with customers. It is surprising to find that almost all these Starbucks are bustling with business, even when considering the nature of this highly café-saturated commercial area. What is so unique about Starbucks? The answer lies in its differentiated "customer experience."

The coffee chain's loyalty program "Starbucks Rewards" and its "Siren Orders" helped cement public perception of their stores as the quintessential hangout spot. Starbucks Korea issued its first Starbucks Card in 2009, expanded the service through mobile apps in 2012, and in 2014 launched its "Siren Order": an O2O (online-to-offline) app that allows customers on the go to remotely order and pay for food and beverages in advance before picking them up. The number of accumulated "Siren Orders" reached 100 million as of 2019, accounting for 22 percent of total orders. The success prompted Starbucks Korea to innovate its IT services to constantly provide new customer experiences. Video smart panels at its drive-throughs allow for easier orders, and "My DT Pass," which provides an automated payment system by reading license plates, shortens the wait time for customers. "My DT Pass" wait time averaged at around 1 minute 40 seconds, whereas that of other drive-throughs stood at 2 minutes 40 seconds. This combination of service and technology boosted the number of "My DT Pass" members to over 500,000 within nine months of service.[1] The root of this bold digital innovation lies in customer experience. By continually agonizing over how to provide a more enjoyable customer experience, Starbucks grabbed the top spot on the Korea Customer Surprise Brand Index (K-CSBI).

The demand for coffee may be the same, but the buying route, process and the experience differ from person to person. Particularly in this digital age, the channels for customer experience are truly diverse, and the feelings evoked involve many variables. It has become all the more imperative to identify such variables in advance and preemptively counter them because they cannot all be controlled for. This is an age of customer experience in which companies must quickly uproot any seed of discontent and pave the way toward customer satisfaction. CX is fast emerging as the cornerstone of customer management and, to a greater extent, of a company's overall management philosophy.

Connecting with customers on an emotional level has become an essential factor in creating brand loyalty and securing a competitive edge, as consumers come into contact with a greater number of brands than in the past. A company's bid to create a positive image and personal relations through overall customer experience management is what we call the "CX Universe."

The Concept of the CX Universe

UX, CX, DT and CX

The cognitive response that users experience when using a product or a service is called "user experience," or "UX." CX, the customer experience, expands on the concept of UX. CX is the overall experience process in relation to the various touchpoints that link consumers and companies, such as apps, stores, products and salesclerks. It is the design and analysis of emotions and reactions throughout the process of the customer's experience with the company's product or service. In other words, CX is the customer's collective experience and emotions throughout the process, starting with product or service awareness, leading to purchase, use, repair, disposal and repurchase. CX goes beyond mere "CS (customer service)" by addressing customer dissatisfaction and by providing added value that exceeds expectations; in other words, it enhances the appeal of the product or service. Restructuring in the consumer landscape in recent years has placed online businesses and omnichannel retail

<UX versus CX>

	UX	UX
Users	Target	Consumers (including potential consumers)
Usage process	Focus	Overall process from pre-purchase to purchase, usage and thereafter
Analysis of the user's needs	Goal	Creating the needs of the customer
Defining usage touchpoints	Concept	Collective customer touchpoints
Building touchpoints & interface	Medium	Devising a strategy
Testing and verification	Verification	Setting a KPI (key performance index)
Easier usage	Direction	Identifying and eliminating negative experiences

at its center, with CX rapidly developing and focusing more heavily on the digital realm.

Redesigning an existing business model on a digital basis to create added value for the customer is called "digital transformation," or "DT," and when emphasis is placed on the experience of such a transformation, the term "DX" can be used. DT, a hot topic in the corporate world, and its related advancement have thrust CX into the limelight in almost all aspects of business innovation, breaking boundaries between what is online and offline. A differentiated

CX has become critical in designing a competitive strategy, especially when targeting Generation MZ, who are more familiar with experiential marketing. Unlike in the past when companies increased their profits through products with a technological or competitive edge, and through aggressive marketing, the current age of complex and multilayered customer experience requires that companies consider a number of factors – corporate culture, manpower, and R&D investment – while focusing on customers. The customer experience encompasses both direct and indirect, as well as virtual experiences, with the direct experience branching off into explorative, usage and purchase experience, and usage experience again divided into shared and resale experience.

Defining the "Universe"

Marvel characters are not only heroes individually, but also as a collective group, as depicted in the *Avengers* series, sharing an interconnected world within the "Marvel Cinematic Universe," or "MCU." It is a source of royalties and an invincible fandom, transcending a simple assemblage of heroic characters. We add the term "universe" to CX to underline the need for a company to build customer relations through CX, not just through individual experiences, but by sharing a distinctive universe.

We are all aware that it costs much less to turn existing

Marvel

The Marvel Cinematic Universe (MCU), the most famous of all cinematic franchises. Each superhero and their fans share a common perception of the MCU.

customers into regulars than to find new customers. Studies have shown that customer satisfaction, when it exceeds a crucial tipping point, significantly encourages repurchasing behavior.[2] Emotion is what tips the scale. A company needs to identify a brand philosophy that exceeds standard satisfaction to augment customers' positive emotions. The "CX Universe" becomes a key strategy in gaining the upper hand only when all these aspects synergistically come together to create the shared universe, rather than just remain an accumulation of customer experiences.

CX is a road that winds through trust and immersion, heading towards loyalty. This road does not end in a cul-de-sac but loops around and begins anew. Each repetition solidifies brand loyalty and evolves into a unifying philosophy.

These values represent a worldview shared by individuals and the collective group, as well as a belief system held by each individual and by society as a whole. Usually when an existing worldview faces challenges, another emerges to resolve the issue and to provide a vision for a new era.

For example, a Tesla vehicle, often called a large computer on wheels, sends real-time interior and exterior sensor-derived data of the driver to Tesla's server, such as placement of the driver's hands on the wheel and driving habits. This data is then used as a reference to upgrade the product's performance and to help design subsequent models. Tesla immediately analyzes the data which helps improve the system. As they send more and more of their own data, Tesla drivers, captivated by the appeal of the self-driving car, feel a sense of pride knowing that they are playing a part in making a safer autonomous vehicle. This enhances a feeling of self-efficiency and a sense of belonging, and at the same time establishes the "Tesla Universe," creating a virtuous circle.

Such brand philosophies are not exclusive to giants such as Marvel, Tesla, Apple and Samsung Electronics. We hope to see some day a "Gimgane김가네 Universe" for the gimbap franchise, or a "Cleantopia크린토피아 Universe" for the dry-cleaning chain. Let's take a look at the goal and implementation strategies.

The Goal of Establishing a CX Universe

Goal 1: Provide a seamlessly smooth experience

The first goal of the CX Universe is by far providing a "seamless" experience. The word has been used to describe product design and physical properties with no trace of seams or joints. In this digital age, the term has become a prerequisite for the overall online and offline experience, including accessing the Internet, e-commerce and secure mobile connections.

What has made Netflix so different from other VOD services? The answer lies in "marathons." Netflix scratched an itch to view a complete series from beginning to end, without the sporadic interruption of ads or episode recaps. It took a gamble and opted to upload original drama series or television shows in their entirety, departing from the norm of weekly uploads, and thus instigated remarkable changes in viewing patterns. Terms such as "marathons" and "binge-watching" became common parlance in reference to attempts to watch a complete series in a single sitting within 24 hours of release, creating an entertaining way for viewers to watch dramas of their choice and spawning a cultural phenomenon. This exemplifies the value of uninterrupted service sought by today's consumers.

Google's "Shoploop" has grabbed the attention of mobile video shoppers. The brainchild of Area 120, Google's internal R&D startup, the seamless service displays product tutorials and reviews, uploaded by influencers on social media, containing embedded links to allow viewers to purchase the goods. It cuts through the hassle of jumping from one app or website to another and has been lauded as an effective integration of e-commerce and advertising. Shoploop users gain access to helpful tips and reviews from others who have previously experienced the product while reserving the opportunity to make a purchase without actually having to visit the store.

Providing such a fluid experience requires extensive technical support and integration as well as detailed planning. A seamless experience is only possible with the full backing of the latest in behind-the-scenes technology that helps identify and preemptively eliminate customer pain points.

Goal 2: Here, take my data

More data allows for better CX. To that end, currently thriving companies are pushing to collect a copious amount of customer experience data. Finding out what the customer wants and how they feel have become prerequisites for corporate growth. And the trend is by no means limited to IT and digital companies.

GPS navigation has become such an integral part of our daily lives that one can hardly remember a time when cars didn't have a GPS device on board. Its benefits are indisputable as the system not only tells you where to go, but also warns you of heavily congested areas and suggests alternative routes. SK Telecom's mobile GPS app "T Map" goes one step further: it offers drivers discounts on their auto insurance premiums based on their driving habits. If you go over the speed limit or come to an abrupt stop one too many times, you are no longer eligible for the discount. Data on such driving habits is exceedingly personal. If the driver can receive more benefits by disclosing his or her driving patterns, then he or she willingly agrees to disclose the information to the company. As such, "What benefits can one gain from which experience?" should be the focus in the design of any CX.

Incheon International Airport, Asia's seventh busiest airport by passenger traffic in 2019, will introduce parking robots. Hyundai Glovis is currently developing an automated parking system, slating a soft launch for 2021. This is indeed welcome news for those who have had to drive round and round to find a spot in a packed airport parking lot. The customer leaves the vehicle at the designated "Pick-up Zone," where it will then be towed by a parking robot, which will dramatically slash parking times. The robot will also fetch the car immediately upon one's return home from abroad, allowing for speedy pickup. The client will of course have to give personal data, including license and registration number and mobile phone number, to enjoy this benefit.

Goal 3: Provide a novel and interesting experience

Millennials, who have embraced experiential marketing, are emerging as the driving force among today's consumers, prompting companies to step up their game in how they structure the type of experience provided. To begin with, companies need to offer a one-off event that provides a novel and interesting experience, breaking away from daily routines.

If a store dares you to grab a pair of kicks placed on a shelf three meters above the ground, would you go for it? When Adidas opened its D Rose Jump Store in London in 2015, it not only grabbed the attention of NBA point guard Derrick Rose's fans, but also provided a rare opportunity for its customers and for the brand itself. The concept may seem old school, but nevertheless Adidas was able to collect a wealth of information with its multiple cameras placed around the pop-up store, including its customers' age, gender, jump ability and their varied responses. If operational experience is limited to past incidents, experience data is all the more valuable to companies because it sheds light on the motives behind consumer behavior.

Companies are also opting for concept stores that go beyond sales and deliver a brand experience. Samsung Electronics unveiled the "Dacor House"데이코하우스 in 2019 to showcase its line of premium built-in kitchen appliances at its Daechidong branch, located in an affluent residential district in the Gangnam area. The Dacor House is a showroom that displays its high-end products in an opulent setting. Rather than selling the products, it operates only nine tours a day for clients who have made reservations in advance, offering them a chance to experience a kitchen worth as much as 400 million won ($350,000). Initially open for only VIPs and major dealers, the luxurious suite allows visitors to relish and experience in the flesh an extravagant penthouse that usually graces the pages of magazines like Architectural Digest.

The Strategy to Creating a CX Universe

As they place more emphasis on CX, an increasing number of companies are setting up various teams, divisions, positions and structures to exclusively manage CX so as to better understand their customers and provide them with a systematic response. StyleShare스타일쉐어, a fashion platform startup, has a team in charge of CX, rather than CS; Hyundai Motors has a Customer Experience Department consisting of CRM, service experience and customer care teams. GS Home Shopping also has a Customer Experience Improvement Team.

Then how does a company create a CX Universe? As stated earlier, modern day consumers, optimized for the conveniences that technology provides, demand a seamless customer experience free from conflict or hassle. They make use of multiple mediums in the process that begins with information search, followed by purchase, and then the sharing of the overall experience. They yearn for a smoother, unimpeded experience more than ever before, as more of them are digital natives who are familiar with the omnichannel experience in which there is no border between online and offline. As such, we would like to introduce three strategies to establish a CX Universe that maximizes customer satisfaction and allows for emotional connection.

1. The Minus Strategy: Eliminating Grievances

The CX Universe is not a collection of individual experiences, and therefore requires companies to reflect on the overall lifecycle of a product or service. Eliminating customer pain points that lurk in this process becomes essential for a seamless experience. The reason why companies are aggressively investing in digital transformation is to effectively eliminate such grievances and turn them into customer satisfaction points.

Improving CX through DT began in the corporate sector. Domino's Pizza launched its "Domino Anywhere" project to minimize the hassle in ordering and to resolve wait-time issues. The strategy allows the customer to easily place their orders through any digital means including Twitter, Facebook, TVs and intelligent assistants. Its "Pizza

Tracker" app allows customers to follow along the process of baking and delivery, informing them of the estimated time of delivery. The company's stocks soared on the back of such endeavors to as high as $375.55 as of June 19, 2020, up 3,200 percent from around $11 in 2010.[3] This outstrips gains by U.S. IT companies such as Netflix (2,325%), Amazon (1,967%), Apple (836%) and Microsoft (632%) in the same 10-year period. This is why Domino's is regarded as the model of a successful digital transformation.

Korean companies are also actively incorporating CX. The food delivery service Baemin 배달의민족 launched its fleet of indoor self-driving mobile delivery robots called "Dilly Towers." Baemin's "riders," as the motorbike delivery drivers are referred to, can now deposit their meals into the Dilly Tower located in the lobby of a given building and leave. The robot will then take the elevator and deliver the food right to the front door of the apartment or office. This saves time for riders who often have to wait for customers in the lobby or the first floor for security reasons. This allows for faster deliveries and ensures security at home and in the office.

Getting a new phone may be exhilarating, and yet quite a bother. You have to physically visit the store and wait to receive the device. SK Telecom has launched a concierge service on a trial basis in which its agents deliver the phone to the customer. After choosing a phone online through its

T Direct Shop, SK Telecom matches an agent closest to the customer for delivery and to complete the paperwork. It is an O2O service with which customers can receive services similar to those in SK Telecom stores.

2. The Plus Strategy: Creating new touchpoints

A key consideration that has emerged in the seamless experience is the "Long Tail" theory. It postulates that though each individual action may seem insignificant, when similar actions are combined it makes for a greater impact. It recommends consumers to rethink their purchasing experiences and fill them with new perspectives. It requires companies to focus on minor and seemingly inconsequential experiences to create new touchpoints.

Offline businesses beset by the COVID-19 crisis have carried over to online touchpoints from their limited outlets. Galleries and exhibits, for example, have had to find new ways to reach customers to overcome limitations amid a drawn-out period of social distancing. Art sales are taking place in online auctions, in line with the growing popularity of live commerce, in which buyers participate through YouTube livestreams.

Augmented and virtual reality, once derided as abominable technologies, have found a niche amid the pandemic among remote access service providers.

The automobile industry, in particular, has been enthu-

Kia Motors

The "Kia Play AR" app allows customers to view and inspect in detail any of its vehicles whenever and wherever they want without having to visit a showroom.

siastic about making use of technology to expand customer touchpoints. Kia Motors' "Kia Play AR" app allows customers to view and inspect in detail any of its vehicles wherever and whenever they want. Potential buyers can use the augmented reality app on their tablet PC or mobile phone to examine the Kia Sorento and, for example, change its interior or exterior, the rims on its wheels, and add or remove various options. Automobiles have longer replacement cycles than other products and therefore usually require special events to attract customers. But with AR, carmakers can now attract a higher degree of customer participation. Since its launch in March 2020, Kia is making use of the app as a central tool to support sales operations.

Mobile shopping may be convenient because it is not

constrained by space and time. Still, there are limitations to direct experience. AR and VR technologies allow mobile shopping operators to overcome such limitations. Lotte Home Shopping introduced its VR Street service which allows customers to virtually visit and shop at its stores. Total users reached 4.4 million as of August 2020 and it is increasing steadily. The number of users saw a 50 percent growth in four months between March and June, triple the total of the same period a year earlier. Shinsegae TV Shopping, in partnership with KT(Korea Telecommunications), initiated a VR fitting service in which the customer can apply personal measurements to the products during broadcasts and examine the completed look in 360 degrees, simulating an actual fitting. The VR and AR market, which allows for unlimited customer experience, is seeing continuous growth.

3. The Multiple Strategy: Multiplying data

When customer touchpoints meet personal information, CX becomes invincible. If customers determine that a brand exists especially for them, this becomes the first step to a good relationship and a shared universe. This use of data that silently supports customer experience creates an invisible connection with the loyal customer.

Make-up giant L'Oréal unveiled "Perso," a personalized beauty device, at the world's largest consumer electronics show, CES 2020, in Las Vegas. The company cemented its status as a world leader in consumer goods by showcasing a personalized beauty product that applies the latest technology. The device can formulate on the spot skin products tailored to the user and the environment, illustrating how a traditional manufacturer can reinvent itself as a service provider through digital transformation. The user takes a selfie and the Perso app uses AI to analyze day-to-day skin conditions, wrinkles, air quality, ultraviolet rays, pollution, and the latest beauty trends, and then combines the information to create the optimal toner and lotion. L'Oréal's forays as a beauty-tech company has generated a solid fanbase that shares a distinct CX Universe.

Amazon is planning to expand its Amazon Go convenience stores, once mocked as nothing more than a novelty concept, in airports and theater districts by combining online and offline shopping in an attempt to change the existing distribution market. The stores make full use of the latest technology, such as virtual shopping carts and electronic receipts, to extrapolate smart data such as purchase habits, frequency and period of visits, payment totals, etc., allowing customers to accumulate their digital experiences.

Outlook and Implications

— The CX Cycle and Thick Data

Devotees of Apple and Samsung devices are often snidely

called "fanboys" and "fangirls." But these companies, each of whom has managed to create its own successful CX Universe, will likely consider such fandom as their badge of honor. Customers are convinced that a company's products enrich their lives and provide emotional satisfaction when they embrace the philosophy put forth by the company. This belief is further solidified the more customers use the product and experience its services, leading to return visits and repurchases that bring about the "Diderot effect." Such customers can become "fansumers," willing to provide companies with personal information. Therein lies the theory of the "CX Cycle," which states that providing customers with experience innovation will prompt their return.

Data is the best means by which companies can ascertain customer annoyances without being asked directly, and to accurately identify the customer's unwitting purchase intent. The customer may be silent, but the data is loud and clear. The importance of big data, propounded by pundits for the past decade, is increasingly proving inefficient in spite of its copious investment. Corporate funding on technology and analysis related to big data are usually hit-and-miss. Studies show that an average company sees a return of just 55 cents for every dollar it spends on big data.[4] And as data becomes more readily available, the application of "small data" is emerging as a means to improve upon customer experience along with big data.

"Small data" can be defined as data that places value on characteristic features of the inherently personal data itself rather than generalizing it. Small data, such as the trace and management of personal recognition data, has a larger impact in terms of CX than does big data. "Thick data" is in-depth information that goes a step further, and can be defined as qualitative information that offers insight into the everyday emotional lives of consumers. Such data is subject to study and analysis to seek qualitative information that might be overlooked by big data. Thick data as experiential data deals with data personalized by consumer lifestyle and provides an opportunity to discover consumers' "emotional DNA" that big data excludes.

Humans think not just with the mind, but with the body as well. Companies need to study consumers' day-to-day habits, assign emotions as variables, and infer data from trivial actions. No longer is big data exclusive to digital transformation. Companies need to obtain insight much like a detective in search of clues, subdividing data according to personal attributes. CX is the best tool for finding those clues.

Adobe, the computer software developer that has taken the lead in CX and digital transformation, publishes an annual report on digital trends. According to its *Digital Trends 2020*, two in five (40%) companies that aggressively tackled CX exceeded profit expectations, while among those

<Big Data versus Thick Data>

	Big Data	Thick Data
Subject of Analysis	Resulting consumer behavior	Purpose and motive of consumer behavior
Domain	Mathematics/Analytics	Overall process from pre-purchase to purchase, usage and thereafter
Method of Collection	Through devices and technology	Through human interaction
Method of Analysis	Objective analysis	Deduction and understanding
Building touch-points & interface	Volume and speed	Insight
Testing and verification	Machine learning	Human learning

that did not invest in CX, only 13 percent managed to meet projections. One in five companies (19%) in the Asia-Pacific region placed CX improvement at the top of their projects for 2020, while more than half (57%) replied that they plan to boost CX R&D investments.[5]

Companies seeking to innovate CX need to enhance their digital capacity and take a more aggressive stance toward digital transformation. Improving CX through DT helps secure repurchase customers. Management consultant Michael LeBoeuf says only four percent of dissatisfied clients voice their grievances, while the remaining 96 percent quietly leave. Of the latter, 91 percent never return.[6] Companies must reevaluate their CX if they want customers to return. We emphasize that companies must define CX innovations as their ultimate goal attained through DT.

CX is proactive. It is anterograde in nature, requiring preemptive resolutions to customers' problems even before they become aware of them. In an age where loyal customers are vanishing, CX has become the goose that lays the golden egg in the form of customer loyalty. Innovative customer experience expands the CX Cycle of return visits and repurchases, and fosters the growth of a sprawling universe of a brand's philosophy. Companies seeking to create fandoms and to allow customers to enjoy the expanding of the universe they want with their brand, emulating the success of Marvel, should herald 2021 as the dawn of their CX innovations.

'REAL ME': SEARCHING FOR MY OWN LABEL

If I were a flower, what kind of flower would I be? What color? What brand? Personality tests have recently become all the rage. Popularity in assessments that determine one's MBTI (Myers-Briggs Type Indicator) personality, or degree of "boomerness," or the best-suited college major, reveals a desire to find one's "real" identity in a multifaceted modern society. In an era of "multi-personas," where an individual can don different personalities in different situations, and of "hyper-personalization," where a person can curate such personalities to their liking, the question "Who am I?" becomes difficult to answer. This "Labeling Game" is how we would like to define the constant search for the "me inside me" during a pandemic and social distancing that has heightened our existential anxiety. It is how a person identifies themself under a label as if playing a game, pursuing a lifestyle that typifies the label thus relieving them of any sense of uncertainty about their identity. The Labeling Game not only helps affirm one's idea of the self in real life, but also often evolves into a game of defining one's identity by comparing and sharing it with others. This allows the person to replace the dilemma over their identity with the joys of consumption in daily life.

To the modern individual living in a consumerist society, the ego is not just a philosophical concept. Today's consumers affirm their self-identity by various tests and follow a pattern of consumer behavior that fits their type. This leads to an inverse causal relationship: "because I am buying this brand, I must be this type of person." The Labeling Game illustrates that corporate brands need to convey that their brand identity and that of their targeted customers is a perfect fit. Only when consumers can willingly identify themselves with brands through a two-way dialogue can corporations hope to emerge as leaders of new trends. It may not be an easy task, but the future of a corporate brand rests on this mutual identification.

"What color would my emotion be when I profess my feelings to someone I love? Or when looking at pictures of a special holiday, a delicious meal, or a precious memory?"

Such was the theme of an exhibit that offered an unusual experiential event in which human emotions were extracted and displayed in color. The event was part of the Wooran Foundation's우란문화재단 *Random Diversity* exhibition at its Seoul gallery. It was an emotion analysis experiment using artificial intelligence (AI), in which the subject would look at a self-chosen picture and an Emotion AI computer examined the person's brainwaves and eye movement, translating the feeling into a color. As the person looked at the picture in question, the computer would detect the color to which the person strongly responds and release a corresponding liquid dye into a flask. The public enthusiasm over the event, access to which was limited to online reservations, was such that it led to ticket scalping on social media.[1] People raved about how their emotions, triggered by a picture of their late grandmother or a significant holiday spot, could be translated into specific colors that they could now hold dear. Fangirls and boys in particular were thrilled by the colors created when thinking about their favorite K-pop idols, further driving the hype for the exhibition on social media.

We live in an age where a computer can analyze and translate how we feel into a color. I'm the one who knows myself best, but we constantly ask ourselves, "Who am I? How can I best express myself?"

When COVID-19 began to take hold in early 2020, gripping the world in fear and anxiety, "Planting My Own Flower" 나만의 꽃 심기 appeared as the top search on Korea's biggest search portal Naver. The search was so out of the blue, especially during a pandemic, that some media outlets claimed it was manipulated. "Planting My Own Flower" was actually the name of a personality and trait assessment test in the form of a five-minute game. It began with a relaxing melody and lovely images that asked the user to pick a type of seed, then asked a series of questions that eventually resulted in a type of flower, such as a carnation, sunflower, cherry blossom, etc., that best depicted one's personality. It also suggested the best type of study buddy and most suitable place to study for the user. The test spread by word of mouth and more than 8 million people took part in it over the course of just two days, with nearly 70,000 logging on simultaneously at one point, straining the server's capacity.[2]

The craze over personality assessments swept the nation

Seekrtech, myuniversity test

Personality tests that inform you of your type of flower or the college major best suited to you. Amid a fascination over one's true identity, personality tests have become all the rage.

as social anxiety brewed during the pandemic, with users poring over tests that measured, for example, MBTI, the level of "boomerness," which college major is the best match, or what sandals best represent the user's personality. They were well aware that test results were not definitive representations of their characters. Still, the tests caught on as a means to discover a side of themselves that they were not aware of, and also helped users briefly forget about the fears of the pandemic.

And yet the question remains: why are people so interested in a test that defines their personality? The concept of "multi-personas" as outlined in our 2020 Consumer Trend Insights may well provide a partial answer. In the digital media age, people are swamped by multiple versions of their (and other) selves – of "mes." Sometimes we get lost in the myriad of egos on blogs, and on Facebook, Instagram and Twitter feeds, but ultimately, when we're faced with ourselves, we wish to find our own identity. The manifestation of these various personas has only piqued our curiosity about our own identities and our "real me," drawing emphasis on the importance of these identity games.

In an era of multi-personas, where an individual can don different personalities in different situations, and of "hyper-personalization," where a person can curate such personalities to their liking, the question of "Who am I, really?" becomes difficult to answer. And as we spend more time on our own due to social distancing, each of us is trying to find the answers by ourselves, and not through our relationships with others. When we tackle the dilemma of the "real me," we are inevitably tempted when we hear about a "test" through which we may be able to make an objective assessment of ourselves. We present the term "Labeling Game" to describe how a person living in the modern age of digital technology searches for one's identity, or the "me inside me," in the midst of a pandemic that has exacerbated our existential anxiety. A label is a sign that identifies an object, or a tag to describe a person's character. The Labeling Game allows a person to define oneself under a label, pursuing a lifestyle in a game-like fashion that typifies that label, and thus relieving them of a sense of uncertainty about their identity. In other words, it is a self-preserving mechanism to solidify a fluid sense of identity in an age of multi-personas. The Labeling Game not only allows us to affirm our identities in real life, but also often evolves into a game of defining our identities by comparing and sharing them with others. This allows us to replace the dilemma over our identities with the joy of consumption in daily life.

These tests pose the same questions. What type of personality do you have? How will this affect your lifestyle and your consumer habits? Just who in the world *are* you?

The Concept of the Labeling Game

Labeling: Classifying oneself through the eyes of others

People have always been curious about their identity. Whenever we trace the origins of myths, legends and folklore from eastern and western cultures, we inevitably arrive at the question "Who am I?" The question becomes even more complex in the modern age of cutting-edge digital communication. The definition of one's self is influenced, intentionally or otherwise, by others through digital media. Everyone has some experience or other of writing, editing or deleting their posts or pictures on social media, in response to comments, or even to meet followers' expectations. And once you begin to upload posts in line with such perceptions, followers on social media will come to understand it as your identity, and you will ultimately come to accept it as who you are. If this persists, your own self-perception will deviate from the identity expressed outwardly and accepted by others, potentially giving rise to an identity crisis.

The doubt over one's own image deepens along with the ever-increasing number of non-face-to-face accounts. The multitude of varieties of social media platforms only hastens an identity crisis. "Is it me? Or my feed?" or "Is my social media identity the 'real me?'" In his theory of the "looking-glass self," American sociologist Charles Cooley studied how others' expectations affect our self-image.[3] It states that just as we look at our refection in the mirror, we incorporate how others perceive us or what we believe to be others' expectations of us, into our own self-image. As a result, we are intentionally or inadvertently influenced by others.

The problem is that others' perceptions of us are incoherent. This only adds to the confusion about one's own identity. As a result, the modern individual yearns for a label, or a "tag," that explains themselves, be it through a scientific assessment backed by psychological evidence, or just a fun simple test to kill time.

Game on: the search for identity through play

With the outbreak of COVID-19, people were forced to distance themselves from social activity. No longer able to enjoy gatherings in small groups, they suddenly had to work alone and find ways to amuse themselves. Each of us tried to alleviate the anxiety of isolation by looking for the little joys in life that we were able to control. The Dalgona달고나 craze and social media challenge is a prime example (see Chapter 5, 'On This Roller Coaster Life'). This was how people began to relieve their anxiety through play.

In an in-depth study on "play," Dutch historian Johan Huzinga defined its core element as something "outside the immediate satisfaction of wants and appetites." He emphasized that human culture is driven by the power of play rather than the power of reason or science. With advances in digital technology and the evolution of games, the modern human is a text-book case of "Homo Ludens," i.e., "human at play." As we are all stuck at home, the passion for play has shifted focus onto games that represent the self. In other words, as games become more diverse, people are gravitating towards games that help express the "me inside me," that is, the "real me" of one's identity.

Play usually involves more than one participant interacting under a set of mutually agreed upon rules. Traditional games such as Yut Nori윷놀이 or poker were characterized by competition in which players pitted their skills and abilities against one another. However, in recent years – especially among video games – players tend to "project themselves" into the game. For example, the player becomes "Super Mario" and embarks on an adventure, or becomes a gun-toting warrior to vanquish enemies. The unique power of a game lies in its ability to prompt the player to willingly take part and actively experience the process, ultimately making it a reality.[4]

A growing number of players are choosing games in which they project themselves onto the character, simulate a reality in the virtual world, and in the process gain confidence and a sense of security. They seek to discover themselves through the pursuit of freedom, enjoyment and fictional imagination through relationships within games, unfettered by the duties and responsibilities of the real world. The surge in the number of gamers has pushed the boundaries of play beyond their virtual worlds, penetrating the wider world. The logic and lure of gaming is no longer restricted to escapist entertainment for gamers, but is rapidly immersing users in other diverse areas, such as education, marketing, and PR, actively incorporating digital media's game thinking, problem-solving, techniques and strategies. This "gamification" occurs when gaming aspects cross over into fields that never incorporated play as their core component. As a result, games are playing an active role in the "labeling" process that aids in the search for the "real me."

The Process of the Labeling Game

So how does the Labeling Game work? In other words, what are the procedures for categorizing and defining oneself through play? We can divide them into three major steps.

1. Quantifying

The first step to labeling oneself is extrapolating a category by "quantifying" one's personality types through obtained data and score results from various tests. Specifically, one can answer a set of questions, and with the results identify certain traits within the provided categories. The most prominent test is the MBTI test, which was immensely popular throughout 2020.

The Myers-Briggs Type Indicator is a personality assessment tool based on the conceptual theory proposed by Swiss psychiatrist Carl Jung. The four categories with opposing qualities are: Introversion-Extraversion (E-I), Sensing-Intuition (S-N), Thinking-Feeling (T-F), and Judging-Perceiving (J-P). The test supposes that everyone has a preferred quality from each category, producing 16 unique types. As MBTI fever caught on, especially among the younger generations, mobile messaging app giant Kakao's sales and merchandising division Kakao Makers quickly printed 16 types of T-shirts emblazoned with the four categories. By wearing the T-shirt, a person was declaring the MBTI for his or her personality type. The first batch sold out within a week, prompting the company to print another batch.[5]

Nearly half a million people took the test to measure their level of "boomerness," otherwise known as the KkonDae* Level Test꼰대레벨 테스트, yet further evidence of people's desire to "quantify" their personality types. The test measures one's KKDTI (Kkon Dae Type Indicator), a cheeky parody of the MBTI, through a survey of some 40 questions, classifying them by various types of boomerness, such as "The inebriated Zhang Fei" (one of the generals and major characters from the 14th-century historical novel, *Romance of the Three Kingdoms*), "The quiet assassin," or "The narrow-minded pacifist." Once categorized, users can look back on their past actions and behavior and receive tips on how to overcome their innate boomerness.

The personality assessments of today differ from those of the past that look at blood type or constellations, relying on a more scientific and statistical approach and allowing users to find some peace and to destress as they share their results with others.

---

* The Korean word *kkondae*꼰대 is slang to refer to an older person as being old-fashioned – someone whose outdated way of thinking is often forced on younger people. While the "Baby boomer" generations of South Korea and the U.S. may have their differences, there is enough overlap as regards to perceived know-it-all attitudes and "when-I-was-your-age" reprimanding by members of the older generations that the term "boomer"/"boomerness" (popularized recently in its dismissive usage by younger generations with the expression "OK, boomer") is an apt rendering of *kkondae*.

2. Symbolizing

"Gucci Boy," "Human Chanel," "Human Dior," ...

When you enter the search word "human인간" followed by a luxury brand such as Gucci or Chanel, images of celebrities decked in the designer apparel flood the screen. Girl group sensation Blackpink's Jennie is called "Chanel in Human Form," and actress and singer Bae Suzy is known as the "Human Dior." BTS's V, Kai of idol group Exo, singer IU and rapper BewhY are all known as a "Gucci Boy or Girl." So, if I were a luxury brand, which one would best express me?

In fact, the brand itself is a metaphor. Choosing a brand is a process of trying to discover one's identity. Andy, Anne Hathaway's character from The *Devil Wears Prada*, and her transformation throughout the movie are a prime example. Despite her initial aversion to luxury brands, she enters the world of high fashion and goes through an identity crisis, ultimately coming to accept the reality of luxury consumerism and undergo a transformation. It shows how brands in today's consumer-driven society become a way to express oneself, beyond any preconceptions of their extravagance or ostentation.

This example contains the premise that spending helps to differentiate myself from others. Thus, the brand effortlessly personifies my unique appeal. Such personification can be defined as a method of "symbolizing" personality traits, in contrast with the aforementioned "quantifying" approach. By comparing and affixing symbolic meaning one hopes to find one's own true traits. "Which artist am I most like?" is another test for assessing one's artistic disposition; to identify one's cultural capital through the development of the pertinent resources. The survey begins with "What would you do on a relaxing rainy weekend?" and then asks 10 more questions, such as what kind of book you would buy at a bookstore that you happen to drop by. It ultimately matches you with an artist and tells you your artistic temperament, going beyond a simple description by attaching a special designation. If you turn out to be similar to Mark Rothko, for example, it gives you a quote or a motto best suited for you, such as "Silence is so accurate," followed by an explanation: "you stir people's emotions with a single deep insight, rather than spewing hundreds of meaningless platitudes. You resemble the abstract expressionist giant Mark Rothko." The test explains your artistic inclinations, recognizes your unique viewpoint, and offers a catchphrase that offers a deeper understanding of your identity. Frida Kahlo, David Hockney and Henri Matisse are among the world-class artists that the test can help you to identify with your hidden artistic sense, handing you yet another label with which to express yourself.

3. Sharing and Confirmation

Once you take part in a test that quantifies or symbolizes your "self" by a label, you then proceed to share and confirm the result with others. The final pages of all these tests have icons that let you share the results on Facebook, Instagram or Twitter. These icons allow the user to instantly post the results and share them with friends and acquaintances on social media. Users voluntarily upload results such as "I got a cactus as my plant" or "I most resemble Frida Kahlo" onto their feeds, revealing various facets of themselves and seeking empathy. More than 30,000 posts with the tag #personalitytest#심리테스트 attest to their popularity.

And because the crux of these tests ultimately lies in the act of sharing, assessments that fail to stir empathy are mostly overlooked. The reason for taking part in these tests may stem from curiosity, but it's also just fun to share the results. It can even be more thrilling to wait for comments after uploading the results than it is to read the actual results. As such, sharing them on social media becomes the most important element of this game. It holds significance because with this tool you get to share a side of yourself, to express yourself, and therefore the process becomes a medium to communicate with others who may have different traits. Influencers and the general public alike get to share their interests through "likes" and "comments," ultimately completing the positive feedback loop.

The Labeling Game Expressed through Consumption

To the modern person living in today's society, the search for one's identity is not only a philosophical concept but has also branched out into the field of consumerism. The protagonists of today's consumer society define their egos through the act of consumption rather than self-reflection. So how is this "Labeling Game" affecting modern consumer behavior?

Scholars have pointed out that as products are imbued with personal tastes and preferences in modern society, we no longer purchase goods simply for their practical use but also for their significance in satisfying our desires. In fact, we choose brands that fit our sense of identity as a means to express ourselves, spending beyond our budgets on luxury items to follow the latest trends. But recently there has been a reversal in this causal relationship. In other words, it is no longer a case of "I'm this type of person, so I'll buy this brand," but rather "I'm buying this brand, so I must be this type of person."

French sociologist and cultural theorist Jean Baudrillard observed that a person who wants to belong to a specific group often chooses to purchase items that members of that group will likely buy as a form of expressing his or her desire to belong, which has come to be known in Korea as the "Effet de panoplie," or "Panoply Effect."[6] Just as a child feels like a police officer by wielding toy guns, badges and handcuffs found in a police kit, the modern person often gains a shared sense of identity by purchasing brands advertised by celebrities. The effect of this panoply of objects and brands is the illusion that through such consumption you've become part of a group that uses a set of objects and displays certain brands.

Today's consumer patterns have been affected, intentionally or otherwise, by the Panoply Effect. "The brand favored by European royalty, and Princess Diana in particular." "Items offered as gifts to Kings in the Joseon Dynasty." "Big name brands favored by such-and-such celebrity." Ads and slogans like these entice consumers, offering the illusion that they too can become a member of European royalty, a Joseon King or a superstar by buying the goods. Consumer purchases with regards to the Labeling Game are quite similar to the Panoply Effect.

The phenomenon has existed for quite some time. The difference between the Labeling Game and the Panoply Effect is the subtle change in the groups that consumers wish to join. In the past, these groups included people that consumers aspired to be but had little hope of sharing membership with, such as superstars or the aristocracy. Nowadays, the groups that consumers aspire to join are those that best express one's own identity, so the path to membership and belonging can be easier to follow. This is the reason why endorsements from mini influencers on social media, with whom consumers share a common interest, have more impact than those of prominent celebrities who always seem out of reach. Whereas the Panoply Effect of the past was upward and vertical, today's Panoply Effect, through the Labeling Game, is reciprocal and horizontal.

However, the problem is that in today's digital media-saturated society one's identity becomes more fluid so that one easily loses confidence about one's sense of individuality and what group one can be part of. It is a result of a combination of multiple factors such as the dawn of multi-personas as illustrated above, hyper-personalized marketing, a reduction in relationships caused by the pandemic, as well as anxiety in modern society, which will be discussed in the following section. Ultimately, we can surmise that consumers began focusing on these numerous personality tests to define themselves and the community they aspire to, affirm their identities through the results and share them with others, and furthermore seek out brands and pursue a consumer lifestyle according to these traits.

We always seek to confirm and affirm our idea of the self, by relying on objective indicators and others' acceptance, rather than through introspection. The Labeling Game can be construed as an expression of a social trend to define oneself through data, tests, and metaphors, as consumers find self-examination more challenging.

Background: An Age of Anxiety

Why do people find games that reflect themselves more interesting? Why has it become so important to affirm my identity, who I am? In our introduction we mentioned the characteristics of the digital media era, but when we follow its roots, we face the biggest existential issue of today, which is "anxiety." The bottom line is that a variety of modern-day anxiety, stemming from numerous factors, has triggered an identity crisis, prompting consumers to become wildly excited about all manner of personality tests that address the question "What type of person am I?"

The above-mentioned Labeling Game and Panoply Effect intensifies as one's ego is shaken. It derives from doubt over whether one can successfully overcome the current predicament with one's own means and resources. People are faced with crippling stress and challenges amid COVID-19 and the consequent recession, as well as the turbulent changes in social trends. As the protagonist in control of their own actions, they ask themselves, "What are my strengths?" The pandemic has made everything in their daily lives uncertain and unstable. They are thrown into an unparalleled situation in which they cannot do what they want, nor what must be done, building up anxiety and doubt about themselves.

In his 2004 book *Status Anxiety*, philosopher Alain de Botton states that our fears grow as we compare ourselves with more people that we consider our equal. He says that when we face an unlimited opportunity to communicate with others, the initial cheery attitude gives way to rising resentment, depression and hatred. This is because communication leads to comparisons. In this paradox, de Botton points out that even if we claim to live in a democratic and capitalist society in which anyone can fulfill their dreams, unsuccessful people are considered failures according to a prevailing system of meritocracy.[7]

Universal standards are no longer absolute amid atypical social values. The disparity is widening between individual need and uncertainty about the world at large. The gap in the job market is a case in point. Some 70 percent of the Korean youth are college graduates, and 50 percent of the unemployed are also college graduates. Every one of the 406,000 unemployed is struggling to find work, and yet the reality is that these highly educated unemployed individuals are only being offered unthinkably unstable, bottom-rung, low-income jobs. Offers are no longer available via large-scale open recruitment but only in downscaled and erratic hires, which has all but snuffed out any hope for young people to find quality positions in their lifetime. In other words, the anxiety of the younger generations in the modern era started when the past model of a well-functioning industrial society, which used to confer one's identity and sense of self through work, began to crumble.

"Will my job disappear in the 21st century?" Everyone has pondered on this at some point. Humanity has always been tasked with the age-old problem of balancing advances in technology and the ensuing concerns over the future of employment. From the invention of the first knitting machine in the 16th century, to the automated loom in the 18th century, and to the subsequent Luddite movement against industrialization, people have always been troubled over how automation will deprive them of their livelihood. Modern humans not only find it difficult to land the positions of their dreams, but even when they do succeed, they never know which new technology will emerge to take their jobs away.

Furthermore, social cohesion has deteriorated amid forced social distancing and the advances in "untact" technology. It is even more vexing for those who have grown up in the digital age – "digital natives" – and who have a harder time building relationships and interacting with people than with digital devices. The sense of community is jeopardized with the increase of untact communication. Even Generation Z, who prefer non-face-to-face communication, admit that communication through social media is somewhat mandatory. This is because direct communication methods outside of the digital realm are disappearing. A free flow of ideas, labor and capital in modern society may be the positive outcome of this transformation, but it has also led to pessimism as society becomes more divided and fragmented. A pervading sense of uncertainty has led to a yearning for a certain level of solidarity and fairness as even Gen Zers feel the lack of social cohesion.

In the past, parents and teachers helped guide us in the direction of life's values, and we set our role models by reading biographies of history's great men and women. As the roles of home and society hold less sway over the individual, people no longer feel the need to emulate those great men and women, giving weight to the creed of "Live your own life." While it may be desirable that personal choice has come to the fore and values have diversified, people are still left to their own devices to seek answers to questions such as "What does it mean to be me?" and "What are my strengths? What do I like? What do I want to become?"

But as with the paradox inherent in the philosopher's saying, "Know thyself," nothing is more difficult than to realize oneself. As a result, people who are stumped by the quest of finding and knowing themselves turn to the digital realm, searching for all manner of personality tests that might give them a clue as to who they are.

Outlook and Implications

— Consumers want to identify with brands

Pot-bellied Ironman; Captain America in the form of an inverted triangle; small and lanky Spiderman; thick-necked and rotund Thanos.

These are the four major body types according to bespoke shirt maker Shirts Specter셔츠스펙터, derived from an AI analysis of big data compiled in the Korean market. They categorized the physical attributes in correlation to four characters from Marvel's Avengers series, offering a service that identifies the body type of their bemused customers and then selects the material and design best suited to that type.

Card Gorilla카드고릴라, which offers comparisons and recommendations of credit cards, makes use of MBTI in selecting the card best suited to the user. The ISFJ type, for example, has introverted, sensing, feeling, and judging personality traits, and would prefer debit cards with which the user can easily manage expenses, even if there are less benefits. Thus, NongHyup Bank's "Ryan Cheese" debit card is recommended.

Global giants such as Amazon and Netflix are already taking advantage of the Labeling Game, in which they categorize their customers according to the data and answers they have provided, offering tailored services accordingly. Of

Zepeto

Creating one's own avatar is the digital version of an identity game. Zepeto제페토, an app that lets you create avatars, or another version of you that's slightly cuter and prettier, racked up 140 million downloads in less than a year since its debut.

course, not all businesses need to categorize or compare their customers in the same manner. Still, such concepts can be applied indirectly to their branding and business models, as modern consumers tend to contemplate their own personal traits, preferences and even their identities.

Corporate brands need to inspire a "That's so me!" response from their customers. Even from the very beginning of the digital era, everyone used avatars and characters in some form or another. It was the first digital expression of one's own identity. We have now evolved into creating avatars and characters that resemble ourselves.

Zepeto제페토 is an app that allows users to create avatars that resemble slightly cuter and prettier versions of themselves. It is a 3D avatar app developed with Naver startup SNOW's augmented reality (AR) technology. A user can pose their avatar in other photos or virtual backgrounds and then post the creation on social media. Since its launch in August 2018, its accumulated downloads exceeded 100 million as of March 2019, and expanded to 140 million by July 2020.[8] More than 90 percent of its members are from outside Korea, attesting to its global appeal. With a single selfie or picture one can create an avatar, change its features and hairstyles, and assign it more than 1,000 different expressions. The app enticed teenagers and stimulated their penchant for play, offering not just avatars that resemble them, but also "a digital me that I can freely express." In other words, the company's success lies in developing a technology that allows users to objectively affirm an image of themselves, and, importantly, in offering the tools for anyone to say whenever they want: "This is who I am."

We are no closer to an end to the pandemic. We are in the grips of anxiety, in the throes of socioeconomic turbulence. We are trying not to plague ourselves with thorny questions such as "Who am I?" "What do I like?" and "What makes me get up in the morning?" Rather, we are trying to alleviate some of our burdens through the satisfaction of light entertainment. The Labeling Game embraces the possibility that consumers, together with companies, can seek to reclaim their own significance. In other words, the Labeling Game is a facet of voluntary modern consumer behavior with which people look inside themselves and express their identities. Therefore, brands can hope to lead new trends only when they consistently communicate with their consumers so customers can easily identify themselves with the brands. It may not be an easy task, but the future of a corporate brand rests with this mutual identification.

COWBOY HERO

'ONTACT', 'UNTACT', WITH A HUMAN TOUCH

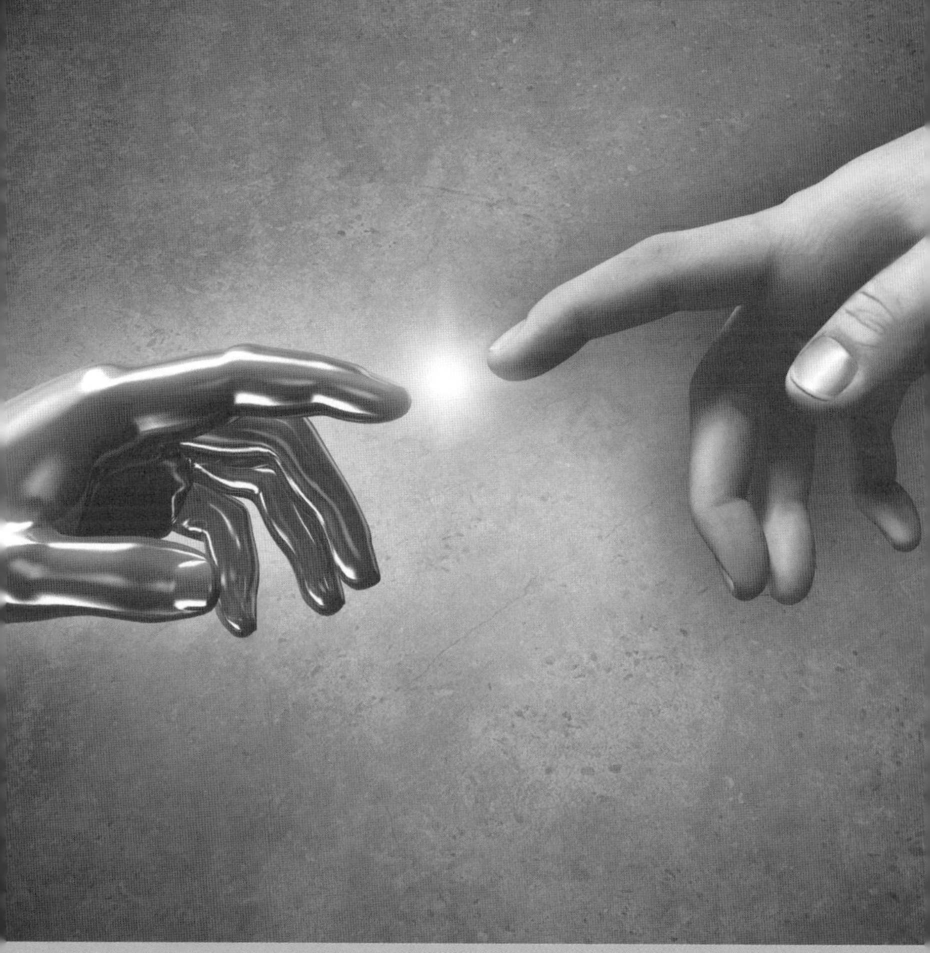

COVID-19 has thrown the spotlight on "untact," or non-contact, technology. However, we have come to realize over time that the future of untact technology lies not in severing or replacing human contact, but in supplementing it. Oddly enough, the need for "Human Touch" has grown. Amid a mishmash of both online and offline markets, Human Touch becomes crucial at "the moment of truth," in which the consumer decides to make a purchase. This is because humans still retain the ability to elicit empathy.
Measures to incorporate Human Touch include: (1) Designing a consumer-centric layout and flow; (2) Enhancing human communication; (3) Adding a touch of the human element to technology; and (4) Mindfulness of team spirit.
Long hours of internet use strengthen the compulsion for human connection, making people feel even more isolated. Video conferencing compounds stress. The greatest challenge will be developing the ability to overcome the loneliness caused by the fear of missing out (FOMO) and the concomitant "digital paradox" that fuels our need for Human Touch.
Human Touch does not suggest a development of technology that simulates actual human touch, nor making technology more human. Its emphasis lies with a conviction that "the human element remains relevant." Human Touch does not require cutting-edge technology, nor is it exclusive to corporate giants. It is the most fundamental practice for any organization to capture their customers' hearts with sincerity. As outlined in the first chapter on "V-nomics," the viral outbreak has forced us to look back on our basic principles. We live in an era of an unassailable pandemic, where technology advances at light speed and trends shift at a breakneck pace. Our final, and possibly most important, keyword to ride out this three-sided wave is a heartfelt and sincere Human Touch.

In the midst of an unprecedented viral outbreak that thrust digital transformation into overdrive, more people are accepting the convenience and efficiency of non-face-to-face services. However, its frequent and repeated use has belied its limitations. An excessive reliance on digital technology diminishes the value of human empathy and physical contact. Human emotions, expressed through empathy and warm physical touch, have become more important than ever. Advances in state-of-the-art technology will ironically reinforce a thirst for warm human sensibility.

As early as two decades ago, American author and futurist John Naisbitt emphasized the importance of human touch in a high-tech era. He states that the ultimate goal for advanced technology should be Human Touch focusing on humanity.[1] Digital transformation needs to place the human element as its ultimate core value. Naisbitt defines his insight on human-centric "high touch" as follows:

What is High Tech / high touch? It is a human lens. It is embracing technology that preserves our humanness and rejecting technology that intrudes upon it. It is recognizing that technology is an integral part of the evolution of culture, the creative product of our imaginations, our dreams and aspirations—and that the desire to create new technologies is fundamentally instinctive. But is also recognizing that art, story, play, religion, nature, and time are equal partners in the evolution of technology because they nourish the soul and fulfill its yearnings. It is expressing what it means to be human and employing technology fruitfully in that expression. ⋯ It is understanding that technology zealots are as shortsighted as technology bashers.

— John Naisbitt, *High Tech / High Touch*

For consumers to become familiar with any given technology, understanding people is imperative. When we defined "untact" as one of our keywords for *2018 Consumer Trend Insights*, we stressed that a comprehensive analysis and understanding of the human element must come first. The untact technology of 2020 is being upgraded to supplement, rather than to isolate or replace, human contact. And as the non-face-to-face era is now in full swing, many companies, faced with the myriad of challenges to its organization's structure and management, are contemplating how best to incorporate a human and emotional element. The reason for our focus on Human Touch, beyond an untact culture, is our attempt to seek answers together to the dilemma of our times. We take a look at the reason why Human Touch is inevitable in an age defined by High Tech/untact technology, its business applications, the background for its emergence, and its implications.

Supplementing Untact Technology with a Human Touch

Why is Human Touch necessary in an age where untact technology and culture is taking hold? The answer to this question becomes evident when we take a closer look at how Noom, an American health and weight management app, incorporated the personal element.

Empathy with a human trainer that AI cannot emulate

Noom, a digital health and fitness app founded in New York in 2007 by a young Korean entrepreneur Saeju Jeong, succeeded in drawing more than $100 million in investments, posting fourfold annual growth from the previous year.[2] Noom's initial goal was to become a company with the most advanced tech in the health and fitness field, and from its launch focused all its research into IT development and predominantly employed engineers on its staff. However, there were limitations to even the most outstanding technology. Users found it difficult to take care of their own health by themselves, despite a sophisticated AI algorithm and attention-grabbing gamified elements. Providing consistent motivation and stimulating interest became vital. In the end, Noom decided to introduce actual coaches, adding a human element. Weight management requires a strong mindset, and an AI-based coaching algorithm couldn't quite take into account the finer details of users' will to work out, their stress levels or their lethargy. As a first step, their coaches e-mailed their members with messages of support and encouragement, sympathizing with their struggles to lose weight, and offered specific answers to their questions about food and exercise, which then resulted in an increase in customer satisfaction. They were acting as pacemakers in a marathon.

The role of the coach became crucial. Noom assigned users a one-on-one coach, along with the assistance of the AI. The idea was for one coach, along with the AI, to manage more than 20 members. Automated responses and repetitive tasks were assigned to the AI, which helped mitigate the workload of the coaches, allowing them more efficient care for Noom's customers. It was a hybrid approach that made use of technology, helping people do what they do best and leaving the technical aspects up to the technology. The role of Noom's coaching staff is to provide a "rich conversation." It raised its subscription fees in October 2015 after adding the coaching element to its AI, providing one-on-one consultations with experts, and still managed to increase its membership. Its users approved of the company's move to provide customized coaches, even at an additional cost, rather than the existing inexpensive standardized service.

Noom's model demonstrates that Human Touch is key to clinching the "moment of truth," in which the consumer decides to make a purchase or continue to receive a service.

Creating the Netflix algorithm, line by line

Companies acknowledged as tech giants all require Human Touch, as machines simply cannot match the emotional sense unique to humans. This is true even for companies such as Netflix, renowned for its highly developed AI-based recommendation algorithm. Netflix has "taggers," who analyze content such as movies, TV programs, and animations. A team of some 50 taggers will watch every film and TV series and tag them with the relevant metadata. These taggers sometimes binge watch content for up to 20 hours a week. Taggers have five years or more of experience in the film or television industry and are required to have deep knowledge and a knack for distinguishing the nuances between different types of content, extrapolate their fundamental qualities, and convey their findings in a concise way. These detailed tasks, unmanageable for AI, can only be tackled by humans with the relevant experience. There are more than 1,000 different types of tags created by these experts. With these tags, video content is then categorized under some 76,000 micro genres and combined with Netflix's accumulated data, creating an unparalleled viewing system.[3] Netflix's extreme classification is often dubbed the "Netflix Quantum Theory," indicating that the secret to the company's superb curation lies not with technology alone but with the people who are behind the finer art of tagging.

As outlined above, Netflix, famous for its AI-based hyper-personalized recommendations, incorporates Human Touch to derive a high level of customer satisfaction. It still uses AI technology, such as machine learning and data analysis, to generate tags and categorize content into micro genres, but its system still needs Human Touch such as analysis from experts to produce an optimal result. The groundwork for quality "taste clusters" can only be completed under the guidance of people with a trained sense for taste and preferences.

Online personal styling service Stitch Fix also uses recommendation algorithms and data science to personalize clothing items based on the customer's preferred style. It does not rely solely on AI, but also on its team of more than 3,000 stylists. The company has chosen to find the ideal balance between AI and the human factor. The stylist, with extensive experience and a sophisticated fashion sense, personally helps choose a style by talking directly with the client. For example, if the client asks for a wedding outfit recommendation, or a chic look for a year-end party among friends, the stylist makes their selection and sends the appropriate ensemble. Often the stylist will leave a memo within the package, advising them to style the overall look in such and such manner. This individualized approach provides the customer with the satisfaction that they are communicating and interacting on a personal level and induces a high level of loyalty. In this way, Stitch Fix inspires customer confidence through scientific analysis of big data, as well as providing the emotional warmth through the human connection with a stylist, thereby enhancing its brand value.

Unlike humans, AI lacks empathy. Chatbots, which many call centers are introducing, may be a convenient technology for companies, yet fail to satisfy customers who have used them—not because their chat technology falls short of expectations, but because AI lacks the ability to understand people. Many scientists laud AI's infinite possibilities. Still, their capacity for empathy seems out of reach. At the end of the day, despite its prominence and advances made, AI will not be able to replace humans when it comes to interpreting human emotions. Neuropsychiatry specialist Jung Hye-shin propounds on the power of empathy.[4]

"Robots and AI need to prove their existence by actively doing their tasks. The human capacity for empathy is a process of understanding others without judgment or calculation," she said.

Customer satisfaction is enhanced through digital technology when the human element and technology is integrated by complementing each other. That is why Human Touch is vital to truly complete a digital transformation. Only by introducing human sensitivities can a company provide a true "customer experience" (as discussed in Chapter 8 on the "CX Universe").

Realizing Human Touch

Then, amid an untact environment rapidly accelerated by the pandemic, how can we incorporate Human Touch? We can accomplish this through four major steps: (1) Designing a consumer-centric layout and flow; (2) Enhancing human communication; (3) Adding a touch of the human element to technology; and (4) Mindfulness of team spirit.

1. Designing a consumer-centric layout and flow

An example of Human Touch-centered design is Portland, Oregon-based Umpqua Bank, which completely restructured its spaces and services according to principles that embody Human Touch. Its "Pretty cool for a bank" slogan attests to their vision to appear less like a bank and more like a friendly neighborhood store that entices customers to stay on its premises for longer periods, allowing for a more varied banking experience in a relaxed atmosphere. The bank's employees undergo customer service training at the Ritz-Carlton and are also trained as baristas at local cafés.

The bank has reimagined each of its branches as a multi-functioning cultural center, even hosting yoga classes. At a time when an increasing number of banks are focusing on more convenient and instantaneous non-face-to-face service, opting for branches entirely devoid of employees, Umpqua has taken the opposite approach of people-centric "slow banking," inviting customers to stay longer and make more use of their services. Customers have responded positively to the bank's strategy to focus more on the human side, breaking from preconceptions that banks are mechanical and inhuman. It enhanced untact technology such as its mobile banking app and self-service kiosks, and at the same time reinforced communication with its clients, providing a high-quality service focused on Human Touch.

Its mobile banking app "Umpqua-to-go," which allows the customer to choose their own personal banker, is a prime example of a service with Human Touch. Using the app, the customer makes his or her choice, browsing through the staff's details, including a self-introduction, photo, profile, and interests. Customers can receive assistance from their personal bankers, frequently communicating with them through audio, video and text messages on their smartphones. It has managed to successfully create a "digital private banking" experience for its customers by integrating a personal element into mobile banking.

Hospitals, which are extremely rational service fields, can

also introduce human sensibility as a core value. Cleveland Clinic in Ohio differentiated itself by offering heartwarming patient care. The respect and integrity shown by the institution toward the struggles of its patients and their family was evident in a promotion video uploaded on its YouTube channel, hitting 5.4 million views. Its small efforts helped the healthcare provider land the No. 2 spot on the World's Best Hospitals list chosen by *Newsweek* in 2019. A hospital that once hovered in the lower end of patient experience satisfaction in the U.S. has now emerged as a symbol of management innovation.[5]

In line with its motto of "Patients First," the Cleveland Clinic realigned its system so that its staff members place patient care at the center. James Merlino, a surgeon and the Chief Clinical Transformation Officer in charge of patient experience, wrote:

Patients were not people; they were diseases that needed to be treated. They became "the small bowel obstruction in the emergency department," or the "SWM with the gunshot wound." Patients and family members who asked too many questions were annoying, and anyone who challenged us was met with aggression. We didn't see our colleagues as people, either.[6]

— James Merlino, *Service Fanatics:*

How to Build Superior Patient Experience the Cleveland Clinic Way"

It illustrates how a system, in which efficiency and technology comes first, can force patients and their families to the brink of inhumanity and even turn colleagues into adversaries.

Such efforts to redesign customer-centered spaces and flow has become a hot topic, not just among hospitals, but among businesses across almost all sectors. Advances in technology may be crucial, but more importantly, companies need to reimagine their structures and practices centered on the customer experience. Only by stepping into the shoes of their customers—seeing, hearing and feeling from their perspective—can companies inspire empathy and capture the hearts of their customers.

2. Enhancing human communication

Opportunities for physical interaction between businesses and customers may have waned, but exchanges through "ontact channels" ("ontact" being another popularized term in Korea for "online untact" interactions) have only heated up, amplifying the potential for personalized marketing. Companies are expanding the scope of customer touch points as even seniors who previously shunned untact technology have grown more accustomed to using digital devices. However, an over-emphasis on the convenience of technology limits empathy and communication with customers. Even when they use untact technology, customers still need to feel sincerity and a warm sensibility.

In order to achieve such goals, companies need to take a friendlier approach, tearing down the persistent divide between company and consumer, between seller and buyer. In this respect, the "ontact" world allows for more access, breaking through any physical barriers. For instance, the public got a glimpse of a conglomerate CEO's human side when they saw him in a *mukbang*먹방 video or a video of him going to the local supermarket. Ham Young-joon, chairman of instant-food maker Ottogi오뚜기, gained attention when he appeared on his daughter's YouTube channel in a *mukbang* video. He also uploads videos on recipes about ideal combinations for his company's products, or promotions for its latest brands. In order to communicate with its consumers, Oriental Brewery's오비맥주 lager brand "Cass" collaborated with the celebrity chef Baek Jong-won to produce its "Beer Class 101" series on its YouTube channel, in which Baek discusses the optimal ratio for a soju and beer cocktail. Kyochon교촌, a leading fried chicken franchise, also announces its latest news and reaches out to its customers through self-produced content on its YouTube channel, such as "Kyochon ASMR."

In the wake of a second wave of COVID-19 that forced gyms and fitness clubs to temporarily shut down, personal trainers took their sessions online, encouraging members to keep up with their workouts. Sports brands are also beefing up their online promotions to keep in touch with their customers. Yoga and athleisure wear maker Lululemon Athletica began livestreaming their yoga classes on Instagram when they could no longer hold sessions at their stores. Yoga instructors who acted as the brand's promoters host these online sessions and upload "home tutorial" videos on their Instagram accounts. Sports brand Dynafit다이나핏, for example, uploads the "Dynafit Elite Academy" series on its YouTube channel, demonstrating simple at-home exercises.

The coronavirus prompted a surge in the use of social media and shed light on the importance of two-way communication and marketing for ontact platforms. According to Twitter's July 2020 survey, 45.8 percent of Twitter users replied that their time on the platform increased, while 74.5 percent of YouTube users noted a similar surge. Some 45.1 percent of Instagram users and 39.8 percent of Facebook users replied that they too spent more time browsing through their feeds. Moreover, only 8 percent of those surveyed said social media needs less advertising, whereas 50 percent were favorable toward ads, because they said it reminded them of the pre-COVID "normal." Even amidst a viral outbreak, consumers were actively communicating with companies. This proves that businesses that communicate enthusiastically with customers in spite of the crisis, providing a range of useful information, are more likely to retain consumer trust.[7]

3. Adding a touch of the human element to technology

Businesses are continually trying to inject warmth and human sensibility into technology. Competition is particularly fierce in the field of AI voice assistant technology, which has already seeped into our daily lives. KT utilizes emotional intelligence-based communication that is tailored to the tastes of its users. If the user says that the tone of its "GiGa Genie" AI assistant's voice is too cold, the AI changes its tone to that of the "Friendly Genie." The user can also switch to the "Calm Genie" mode when searching for information such as news. It has tried to stand out among the myriad of rivals by offering AI voices that suit the taste of the user. Others provide a service that changes the voice's tone to mimic celebrities, with the AI learning the vocal and audio data of specified personalities. SK Telecom's "NUGU" incorporated a celebrity alarm function, utilizing the voice of Irene, a member of the famed K-pop girl group Red Velvet. The user can receive various types of alarm bells and wake-up calls in Irene's voice. For example, once the user inputs his or her nickname, Irene will whisper, "Joon, it's time for dinner" or "Darling, time to get up." It is similar to the popularity of GPS voices that gave directions to drivers in regional accents and dialects, rather than the standard announcer-type voices.

Today's consumers, surrounded by digital technology, may be searching for a more human type of machine, i.e., one that is "not quite like a machine." According to KT's analysis of the commands and phrases of GiGA Genie voice assistant users in 2019, the most commonly used terms were emotive expressions such as "I love you," followed by "Hello" and "What're you up to?", as well as "Thank you" and "I'm sorry." This suggests that people expect their voice assistants to take on the role of a friend, or a digital companion.

But then, can technology console humans? There have been many attempts to find the answer to this question. As the pandemic took hold, several states in the U.S. began to provide robot pets to alleviate loneliness among the elderly. States with senior citizens-related departments such as New York, Florida, Alabama, Pennsylvania and others have worked with robotic pet manufacturer Ageless Innovation for the pilot project. It was a success, with 70 percent of participants in the program reporting a decrease in feelings of isolation within a year. Senior citizens, confined to their homes during the pandemic, were able to warmly engage with their robotic companions without assuming responsibilities such as walking the pets or cleaning up after them.[8] The project had successfully created pets through digital companionship technology.

4. Mindfulness of team spirit

Teleworking from home became the new normal ever since the viral outbreak, leaving many to yearn for the times of working with colleagues. Some firms even organized online company dinners to boost staff morale, dining on their own dishes and drinks and chatting away in front of their phones or laptops from home in a group video conferencing session. It was an online alternative to in-person social interaction to maintain a sense of human connection. This new normal has also shed light on concerns about employees' mental well-being. Mindfulness of the workforce becomes paramount as sound mental health directly correlates with productivity. In an August 2019 survey of 671 office workers on work-related illnesses by job search portal Incruit인크루트, 83.9 percent replied that their health had deteriorated since joining their companies. Stress-related ailments were the No. 1 cause of work-related illnesses, specifically depression, insomnia, repressed anger and chronic fatigue.

Such conditions breed "presenteeism" among the staff; in other words, they may physically be at work, but not be able to fully perform their duties. It is more detrimental than "absenteeism," in which employees do not show up for work at all citing health reasons and causing visible losses in productivity. Absenteeism is manageable because it can be detected. Presenteeism, on the other hand, is not so obvious, and therefore often flies under the radar.

When members of an organization suffer from mental duress that diminishes their enthusiasm, conflict ensues within the ranks. Businesses often shore up support for the mental health of their staff through various means, one of which is implementing emotional intelligence (EQ) in leadership. Psychologist Daniel Goleman propounds on the importance of EQ on productivity. At best, IQ makes up for 20 percent of the factors that determine organizational performance, while other forces, such as EQ, wealth, temperament, family education levels and pure luck make up the difference. As such, there is growing emphasis on emotional leadership, emotional intelligence and emotional labor. Emotional leadership requires above all management's thoughtful consideration, customized to each employee. Leaders need to carefully plan various supportive measures such as communication with senior management and among employees, funding for employee gatherings, cultural activities, celebrations for anniversaries, as well as upgrading rec rooms and other facilities to enhance employee welfare. COVID-19 and the subsequent "corona blues" has shed light on the importance of managing employee stress levels.

Background : The "Untact Paradox"

What has caused the paradoxical situation in which the human factor has become more important amid an untact culture that excludes human contact as much as possible? It is because behind the convenience that technology bestows lies the loneliness and isolation of modern people. Has the increase in online connection enriched human relations? Or have we become even more isolated? This depends on how we make use of the Internet. We need to maintain an ideal balance of "not too much and not too little" time spent online. In other words, the "Goldilocks Hypothesis" comes into play.

Most people in modern society find it difficult to disconnect from online activities. Tech giants such as YouTube, Instagram, and Netflix strategically exploit psychological strategies to entice users to stay logged on for longer periods of time. Instagram, for example, delivers endless new content as the user scrolls down. YouTube has an "Autoplay" function that automatically plays the next recommended video. These services hook the user as soon as they log on. App service providers have to lure members to spend more time on their devices because they need to rack up as many monthly active users (MAUs) as possible to maximize profits. In this context, the share of customers' digital screen time will become more important than expanding the share of customer revenue.[9]

Psychologists Andrew Przybylski and Netta Weinstein claimed that the total amount of digital screen time had both a positive and a negative impact on users. According to the Goldilocks Hypothesis, an hour or two of digital screen time was not harmful. However, two or more hours on the smartphone or other digital devices was linked to lower levels of wellbeing. On the other hand, their study showed that no daily screen time among children had in fact a negative influence. In modern society, in which connecting online is routine, cutting off online access entirely will only breed negative feelings of alienation and isolation.

Excessive online connection has triggered a modern compulsion to remain connected. In the past, loneliness was considered an inevitable part of life. Modern people, who can connect with others anywhere and at any time with their smartphones, believe they have the means to mitigate loneliness. This compulsion to stay online has prompted people to constantly connect with others through their devices, rather than taking time for inner reflection. Moreover, amid a perception that it's hip to have all kinds of fun all on their own, people are reluctant to express their loneliness to others.

Digital devices stimulate a desire for interaction with others through social media and amplify solitude in modern society. People sometimes suffer from a fear of missing out (FOMO), borne from their fear of being ostracized. This prompts them to constantly seek a connection with others by uploading posts and pictures on their social media accounts, which, when failing to receive "likes," makes them feel disappointed, leading them to upload even more posts and pictures to seek approval from others. The increase in online activity has ironically amplified a fear of loneliness, creating the "Untact Paradox." The prevalent use of video

As untact video conferencing become routine, an increasing number of people are complaining of fatigue caused by disconnection and isolation, as well as a lack of social cues and non-verbal communication.

conferencing tools such as Zoom and WebEx as a result of social distancing has created a new form of stress dubbed "Zoom Fatigue." An article titled "Why Zoom Is Terrible" published in the *New York Times* in April 2020, stated that Zoom is stressful to those unfamiliar with online video conferencing. Communication is achieved through various means besides standard verbal cues, but also through non-verbal cues, and disruptions in video calls can greatly hamper this process. Trying to identify these social, non-verbal cues on a small screen is very stressful. Moreover, having to look at yourself while conducting a conversation, constantly monitoring your own facial expressions, is also taxing. Psychologists, neuroscientists and computer scientists say the distortions and delays inherent in video communication can end up making you feel more isolated, anxious and disconnected.

According to the Goldilocks Hypothesis, we should be wary of detrimental side effects caused by excessively relying on the convenience of untact technology. Businesses can amplify results by making use of the technology at the right place and time, when prudently combined with offline values. In that respect, Human Touch becomes more relevant in an untact society.

Outlook and Implications

— Human Touch Is and Always Will Be Relevant

Platforms such as Coupang쿠팡 and Baemin배달의 민족, which have become part of our daily lives, are providing hyper-personalized services by collecting and analyzing real-time personal data through digital technology. In the modern non-face-to-face era, new industries such as lifestyle platforms are tasked with attaining customer satisfaction by providing a high level of service through Human Touch.

Starbucks is one such example. Cafés are traditionally a non-digital sector, but as illustrated in our chapter on the "CX Universe," Starbucks succeeded in its digital transformation and retained its lead in a cutthroat market. Its dominance in the red ocean of coffee shops was only possible due to its online strategy called the "Digital Flywheel." The flywheel is a vital component when roasting coffee that helps maintain a constant rotation speed of the coffee roasting machine. The franchise has applied this concept, not just to producing the best cup of coffee, but also to its overall strategy to provide its customers with a faster and more convenient ordering process making use of complex algorithms. Starbucks has reinvented itself as not just a coffee franchise but as a digital company as well. And even with its focus on digital advances, Starbucks still emphasizes Human Touch. Kevin Johnson, CEO of Starbucks, states:

"But we also are finding new ways to use technology and data to really enhance human connection. One of the initiatives we have is our artificial intelligence initiative, called "Deep Brew." And in many ways, Deep Brew, and the focus on machine learning and artificial intelligence, is all about finding ways to help humans have more time to be human … So, it's not about robots to replace baristas; it's about technology that frees up our baristas to better connect with one another and connect with customers." [10]

In other words, the company is not trying to turn Human Touch into some kind of technology, nor is it trying to create a technology that simulates people, but rather is staying true to its creed that "Human Touch is still necessary." As previously stated, the "moment of truth" in the customer's journey, both online or offline, comes when the customer feels a personal connection. The crucial moment at a café comes not when the coffee flows out of the espresso machine, but when the barista brews the coffee and hands it to the customer with a smile. In other words, its essential quality is decided at the "moment of Human Touch."

In fact, Human Touch does not require cutting-edge technology, nor is it exclusive to corporate giants. It is the most fundamental practice for any business reaching out to its customers with sincerity. As outlined in our "V-nomics" chapter, the viral outbreak has provided us an opportunity to look back on our basic principles. We live in an era of an unassailable pandemic, where technology advances at light speed and trends shift at a breakneck pace. It is time to get down to the basics. Our final and most important keyword to ride out this three-sided wave is a heartfelt and sincere Human Touch.

Notes

V-nomics

1 '코로나 바이러스 감염증 −19', 나무위키 검색.
2 소비 · 투자하라고 돈 풀었지만…예금만 109조 늘어 / 매일경제, 2020.07.28.
3 Sadly, One Letter Perfectly Captures the Recovery / Bloomberg, 2020.09.03.1
4 코로나타격 입은 한국 경제, 극단적인 K자형 회복추세 / 세계비즈, 2020.09.07.
5 '풀뿌리 경제' 골목상권, 코로나 재확산에 모든 지표 하락 / 매일일보, 2020.09.17.
6 "코로나19 위기, 강한 기업 더 강하게" / 내일신문, 2020.03.31.
7 通通한 재택근무에 '업무 군살' 쏙~ / 서울경제 2020.03.27.
8 아기상어는 재택상어 뚜루루뚜루~ 5년 만에 매출 11배 비결은 / 조선일보, 2020.09.22.
9 교사 70%, 포스트코로나 시대 새로운 수업 방식 기대 / 에듀동아 / 2020.08.19.
10 모든 삶이 '디지털'로 옮겨 온 시대…'라이프 플랫폼' 성장 공식은 / 테크M, 2020.07.03.
11 맥킨지 "코로나19가 美 전자상거래 10년 앞당겼다" / 오피니언뉴스, 2020.08.10.
12 대세가 된 ESG투자…모르면 돈 못 법니다 / 조선일보, 2020.09.20.
13 〈위축된 삶, 지속될 영향, 실용적 적응: 코로나19 시대, 소비자 생활과 소비 활동에 대한 영향과 전망〉, 한국리서치, 2020.06.12.
14 〈위축된 삶, 지속될 영향, 실용적 적응: 코로나19 시대, 소비자 생활과 소비 활동에 대한 영향과 전망〉, 한국리서치, 2020.06.12.
15 선생님 10명 중 8명 "원격수업으로 학습격차 커졌다" / 조선일보, 2020.09.22.
16 박찬욱에게 영화를, 커리에게 농구를 배운다고? / 조선일보, 2020.09.12.
17 코로나19 이후 강해진 혐오…10명 중 9명 "나도 혐오 대상 될 수 있어" / 서울경제, 2020.06.23.
18 공간이 만드는 세상, 공간이 만드는 미래 / 대학신문, 2020.09.13.

Omni-Layered Homes

1 코로나發 침체에도 위생 가전은 날았다 / 서울신문, 2020.03.13.
2 #랜선집들이, #홈스타그램…2030에게 '집 꾸미기'는 무엇일까요 / 한겨레, 2020.07.31.
3 가구업계, 온라인 매출 36% 늘었다 / 한국경제, 2020.08.23.
4 인테리어 플랫폼 '오늘의집', 누적 앱 다운로드 '1000만' 돌파 / 플래텀 / 2020.05.19.

5 "오래 살아온 공간에는 상처가 있다"…듣는 순간 격공하는 김영하 작가 현실어록 4 / 인사이트, 2018.12.07.
6 미술작품 구독 서비스 스타트업 '오픈갤러리', 상반기 매출 71% 증가 / IT비즈뉴스, 2020.08.15.
7 '홈요가'를 넘어 '홈짐'까지…각양각색 홈트세계 / 한국일보, 2020.07.16.
8 자주, 집에서도 피부 관리 돕는 '홈뷰티 기기' 첫 선 / 매일경제, 2020.04.03.
9 1.6조 홈뷰티기기 시장 잡아라…LG전자, '피부과학 자문단' 운영 / 한국경제, 2020.04.21.
10 "해외여행 못 가도, 퇴근 후 남의 집이 이탈리아 돼요" / 조선비즈, 2020.08.11.
11 "이러니 서울 집값 오르나"…서울 출퇴근 길바닥에 1시간 31분 / 서울경제, 2020.07.30.
12 코로나19로 시간 • 장소 자유로워진 유연근무제 정착…대기업 4곳 중 3곳 탄력적 근무 현재 실시 중, 근무시간보다 성과 중심의 평가제도 정착 필요 / 매일경제, 2020.08.28.
13 재택근무는 장거리 연애와 같다 / 조선일보, 2020.09.11.

We Are the Money-friendly Generation

1 빈곤의 역설, '플렉스'가 뜬다 / 조선일보, 2019.12.20.
2 알바비로, 용돈으로 flex…명품 사러 무신사 가는 10대들 / 아시아경제, 2020.03.23.
3 한정판에 열광하는 소비자들…'드롭''래플'을 아십니까 / 조선일보, 2020.03.07.
4 카카오뱅크 '저금통' 13일 만에 100만 좌 돌파 / 파이낸셜뉴스, 2019.12.24.
5 청년들 빚투 광풍… 주식 신규계좌 • 金투자 절반 이상이 2030 / 조선일보, 2020.07.27.
6 MZ세대의 요즘 재테크 / 일간스포츠, 2020.06.17.

Best We Pivot

1 경영 전략? '전략'부터 이해하자 / 머니투데이, 2011.11.14.
2 변화되는 소비자 행태, 피버팅도 고려하자 / 스타트업투데이, 2020.06.19.
3 돌돌 말아서 집 앞까지 택배로…'롤팩 매트리스'가 온다 / 아주경제, 2020.07.26.
4 '팝업시티(Pop-Up City)'를 허하라 / 인터비즈, 2020.07.22.
5 이동건 마이리얼트립 대표 "코로나가 서비스 다양화 기회 됐어요" / 한국경제, 2020.08.18.
6 크리에이트립, '한국직구 방송' 오픈 / ZDNet Korea, 2020.04.14.
7 지능형 기업으로 거듭나기 / CIO Korea, 2020.08.10.
8 포스트 코로나의 글로벌 비즈니스 환경, 적자생존일까 구조변화일까? / 뉴스페퍼민트 (원문: The Economist), 2020.04.06.
9 韓 대표그룹 주력 계열사 15개중 11곳 상반기에 매출 줄었다 / 중앙일보, 2020.08.18.

10 대기업이 스타트업보다 잘할 수 있는 것들 / 뉴스페퍼민트(원문: Harvard Business Review), 2013.02.01.
11 '샤워실의 바보', 〈한경 경제용어사전〉, 네이버 지식백과 검색.
12 스피드 경영–위즈에어(헝가리 저가항공) • 스타십테크(영국 로봇 배달 기업)…코로나를 기회로 / 매경이코노미, 2020.07.03.

On This Roller Coaster Ride

1 지코 '아무노래'열풍으로 본 '밈 컬처'의 시대 / 한국경제, 2020.02.21.
2 동아오츠카, '오로나민C볼단' 모집에 소비자 관심 / 글로벌이코노믹, 2020.07.26.
3 MZ세대 잡아라…식품업계, 소비자와 논다 / 머니투데이, 2020.07.22.
4 '깡' 열풍 뜨겁네…농심 '깡' 시리즈 한달 매출 100억 돌파 / 조선비즈, 2020.08.12.
5 러마, 웨이브, 키트…어른은 모르는 10대들의 놀이터 / 조선일보, 2020.07.08.
6 '지금은 생방송 중'…라이브 커머스 폭풍 성장 / 국민일보, 2020.08.02.
7 MZ세대는 왜 '곰표'에 열광할까 / 더스쿠프, 2020.08.10.
8 박지혜 • 설경옥 • 김지혜, "아동기 부정적 부모양육 경험과 대학생의 문제음주의 관계에서 충동성과 대학생활 음주 중요성 인식의 매개효과", 〈한국심리학회지: 발달〉, 31(2), 2018, 125~144쪽.
9 농심 '앵그리 RtA' 화끈한 출발…2주 만에 400만 개 팔려 / 매일경제, 2020.02.04.
10 "의식의 흐름대로"…CU의 대충 이벤트, B급 감성으로 매출↑ / CNB저널, 2020.08.19.
11 무신사 • 지그재그 • 29CM…"백화점 안 가는 MZ세대 공략해 떴어요" / 조선비즈, 2020.01.25.

Your Daily Sporty Life

1 서핑에 빠진 한국 5년새 400% 성장! 클룩, 서핑 • 수상 카테고리 오픈 / 투어코리아, 2020.06.04.
2 골프장, 90년생 '큰 고객'으로 급부상 / 이뉴스투데이, 2020.05.23.
3 룰루레몬, BMW 시총 제쳐…코로나가 바꾼 세계 주식시장 / 한국경제, 2020.08.09.
4 부장님만 등산을 좋아하는 건 아니랍니다 / 경향신문, 2020.06.14.
5 "등산도 힙하게"…레깅스 • 크롭톱 입고 인증샷 찍는 MZ세대, BAC에 꽂히다 / 뉴데일리경제, 2020.06.25.
6 코로나블루 우울함 확 날려줄 명상앱 / 매경이코노미, 2020.04.17.
7 男女 일상복 영역 들어온 레깅스 / 아시아투데이, 2020.07.30.
8 젊을 때 내 몸을 기록한다! 바디프로필 촬영 인기 / 조선일보, 2020.08.06.
9 앱으로 기록 공유…슬기로운 운동생활 / 동아일보, 2020.06.01.
10 '환경 챙기는 게 우선이다'…컨셔스 트레킹족 주목 / 매일경제, 2020.06.01.

11 앱으로 만난 사람들…수영반 회원들…서로 응원하며 달렸다 / 조선일보, 2019.04.29.
12 김다영, 『여행의 미래』, 미래의 창, 2020.

Heading to the Resale Market

1 "중고거래를 선호하는 이유 | 중고거래 어디가 좋을까?", 유튜브 채널 'Miner마이너'(www.youtube.com/watch?v=mu2o-wyO1SQ)
2 중고거래 앱 당근마켓…'직거래'로 여성 사로잡다 / 여성신문, 2020.05.14.
3 BTS도 '쿨거래'…일상의 놀이 된 중고 거래 / 조선일보, 2020.01.18.
4 민트급 • 풀박? 거래 용어 꽉 꿰고 중고 거상 되어보자 / 한겨레, 2020.07.30.
5 "요즘 누가 카페에서 알바해요"…'진격의 중고앱', 코로나로 잃은 알바 자리 대체한다 / 한경잡앤조이, 2020.08.04.
6 1020세대 '리셀' 수익 쏠쏠…중고거래 플랫폼 진화 / 매일경제, 2020.06.19.
7 중고거래 최고 인기 굿즈…스타벅스 '서머레디백' / 스카이데일리, 2020.08.25.
8 "먹다 남은 피자 사실분~"…별걸 다 파는 중고거래 시장 / 매일경제, 2020.08.12.
9 중고시장 리셀바람…"저렴한 가격? 핵심은 유니크야" / 국민일보, 2020.06.27.
10 "스니커즈는 어떻게 최고의 투자 아이템이 되었나", 〈폴인트렌드〉, 2020년 02월호.
11 중고거래 빠져드는 이유 '돈'이 아니다 / 머니투데이, 2020.06.05.
12 2020년식 아나바다 / allure, 2020.05.09.
13 "먹다 남은 피자 사실분~"…별걸 다 파는 중고거래 시장 / 매일경제, 2020.08.12.
14 신발 샀는데 쓰레기가…공정위, 중고거래 앱 상반기 중 조사 / 조선비즈, 2020.05.03.
15 '리테크'에 빠진 MZ세대…"스니커즈는 가장 핫한 돈" / THE PR, 2020.08.12.

Everyone Matters in the 'CX Universe'

1 스타벅스 '마이 디티 패스' 가입자 50만 명 돌파 / 연합뉴스, 2019.03.18.
2 질 그리핀, 『충성고객 이렇게 만든다』, 코리아리서치센터 옮김, 세종서적, 1997.
3 '도미노피자' 주가상승률 왜 애플, 아마존보다 더 높을까? / 조선일보, 2020.08.28.
4 "Enterprises Struggling to Derive Maximum Value from Big Data(빅데이터 가치 극대화의 어려움)", Wikibon, 2013.09.19.
5 꾸미는 것을 멈추고, 쇄신이 필요한 'CX' 개선 / 블로터, 2020.06.17.
6 마이클 르뵈프, 『착한 고객』, 김승억 • 이미숙 옮김, 교보문고, 2010.

'Real Me': Searching for My Own Label

1 色, 찾아드립니다 / 조선일보 / 2020.08.13.
2 갑자기 실검 1위? 심리테스트 '나만의 꽃 심기'는 어디서 등장한 걸까? / 서울경제,

2020.03.28.
3 이동귀, 『너 이런 심리법칙 알아?』, 21세기북스, 2016.
4 권보연, 『게이미피케이션』, 커뮤니케이션북스, 2015.
5 "넌 무슨 유형이야?"…'진부한' MBTI 검사는 왜 2030을 사로잡았나 / 이데일리, 2020.06.21.
6 장 보드리야르, 『소비의 사회』, 이상률 옮김, 문예출판사, 1992.
7 알랭 드 보통, 『불안』, 정영목 옮김, 은행나무, 2011.
8 네이버는 국내용?…해외 이용자 1억 명 넘는 서비스만 4개 / 한국경제, 2020.01.21.

'Ontact', 'Untact', with a Human Touch

1 존 나이스비트, 『하이테크 하이터치』, 안진환 옮김, 한국경제신문사, 2000.
2 미국이 주목하는 '코리안 파워' 정세주 눔 대표 / 〈포브스코리아〉, 202003호, 2020.
3 "언택트 시대의 콜센터, 기술&감성 융합한 '하이터치'로 대응", 한국능률협회컨설팅 블로그(blog.naver.com/kmacforever/221989506838), 2020.06.04.
4 이성적 공간을 감성적으로, '클리블랜드 클리닉' / WK마케팅그룹, 2020.03.02.
5 제임스 메를리노,『환자의 경험이 혁신이다』, 박재영 • 김인수 옮김, 청년의사, 2015.
6 "코로나19 이후 SNS 사용 급증…양방향 마케팅이 대세" / 이데일리, 2020.07.09.
7 "어르신 코로나 고독감 달래주자"…뉴욕주 등 반려동물 로봇 보급 / 한겨레, 2020.08.12.
8 흔들리는 직원 멘탈/ CIEF EXECUTIVE, 2020.07.23.
9 비벡 H. 머시, (2020), 『우리는 다시 연결되어야 한다』, 이주영 옮김, 한국경제신문, 2020.
10 "스타벅스 AI '딥 브루', 생각과 다른 기술일세", 데일리트렌드 웹진, 2020.01.22.